A SHEEPDOG NAMED OSCAR

A SHEEPDOG NAMED
OSCAR

Love and Companionship

in Rural Ireland

By Dara Waldron

Doppel House Press

A Sheepdog Named Oscar
Love and Companionship in Rural Ireland
By Dara Waldron

DoppelHouse Press, 2025

Text and images © Dara Waldron, 2025
except where noted.

Book Design: Carrie Paterson

Publisher's Cataloging-in-Publication Data

Names: Waldron, Dara, author.
Title: A sheepdog named Oscar : love and companionship in rural Ireland / by Dara Waldron.
Description: Los Angeles, CA: DoppelHouse Press, 2025.
Identifiers: LCCN: 2025932729 | ISBN: 978-1-954600-29-4 (paper-back) | 978-1-954600-31-7 (ebook) | 978-1-954600-37-9 (audiobook) Subjects: LCSH Waldron, Dana. | Border collie--Ireland--An-ecdotes. | Grief. | Pets. | Human-animal relationships. | BISAC BIOGRAPHY & AUTOBIOGRAPHY / Memoirs | LITERARY COLLECTIONS / Subjects & Themes / Animals & Nature | LITERARY COLLECTIONS / European / English, Irish, Scottish, Welsh | LITERARY COLLECTIONS / Subjects & Themes / Places Classification: LCC RM931.D63 W35 2025 | DDC 636.7--dc23

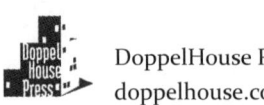

DoppelHouse Press | Los Angeles
doppelhouse.com

FSC
www.fsc.org
MIX
Paper | Supporti g
responsible forestry
FSC® C00501

For Anton

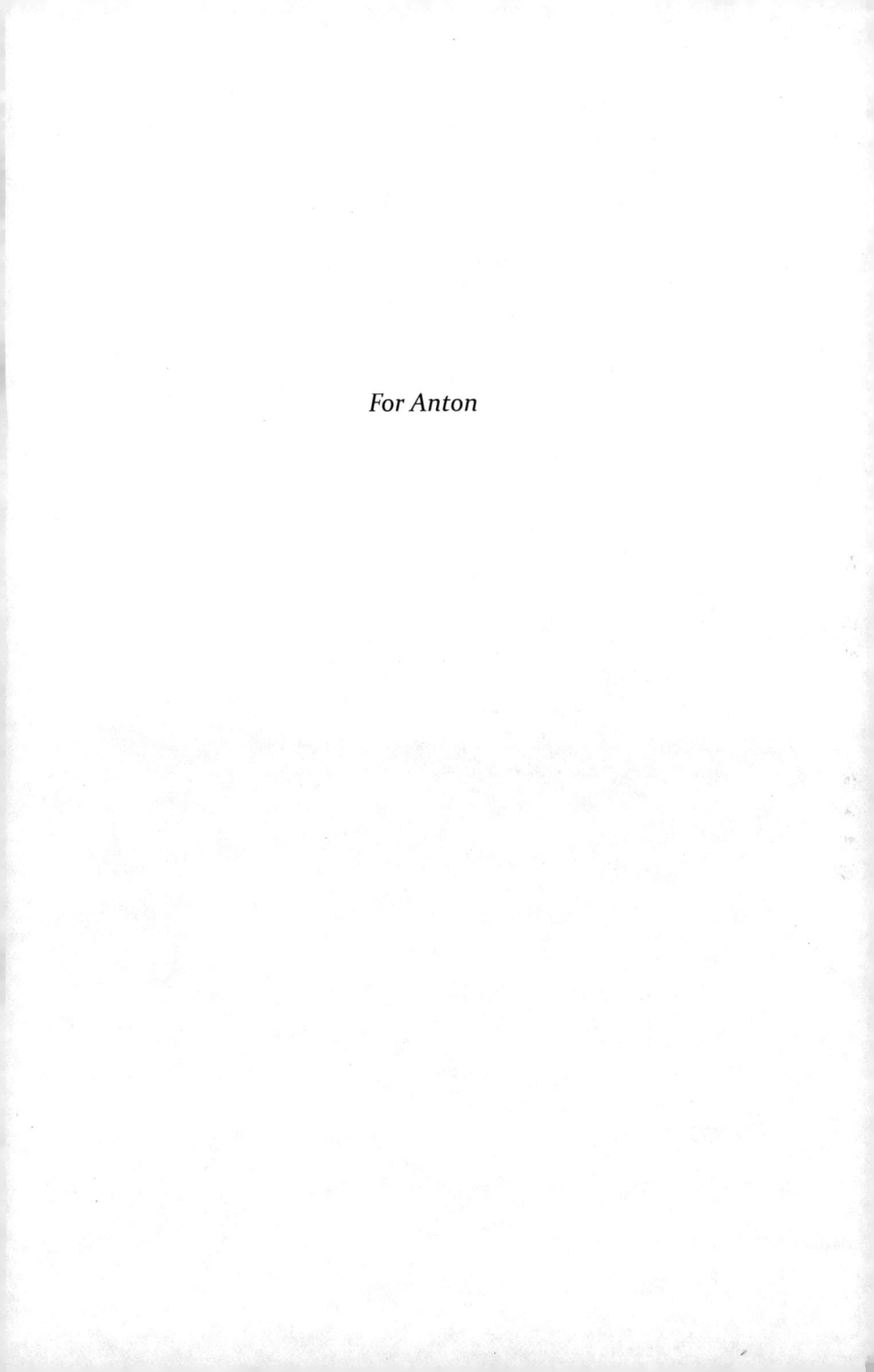

*There is no limit to the extent to which we can
think ourselves into the being of another.
There are no bounds to the sympathetic imagination.*
— J. M. Coetzee

Love, and do what you will.
—St. Augustine

ONE ⁑ THE RESCUE ACT

On the weekend, the habits of my toddler son Anton began to solidify. During breakfast he would turn and utter the words "Finding Nemo." Tired and sometimes half asleep, I'd seek out a VHS copy of the film. We'd sit back together and watch the movie from beginning to end. At some point I estimated we had watched the film over a hundred times. It was difficult to countenance a child's need to watch a movie over and over, to a point of banality. But he did. We both did. Some years later a critique of the film captured my attention: it's about separation anxiety. Nemo is a child fish, a young male who ventures off with Dora, a female of another species. They get lost. Nemo escapes capture and makes it home to be reunited with his dad. Perhaps Anton was experiencing something like Nemo? In his development, he was asserting independence. By repeatedly watching the same movie with me at his side, he was learning to cope with being on his own.

DARA WALDRON

The story that unfolds in the pages to follow is about being alone and counteracting it. It is a story about interspecies companionship, love, and loss. A sheepdog named Oscar becomes my companion. He came into my life on the first anniversary of my father, John Waldron's death. Somehow, I believed that Oscar found a way to me. Our lives intersected at a time when he was a stray in need of a home, and I was astray and in need of a friend. He didn't ask questions when doubts and uncertainty swirled around in my head. My family lineage is typically Irish. Both my parents left Ireland for Manchester in the 1970s to work in a British hospital. They returned from England to take over my grandfather's practice soon after I was born, (my grandfather Tony Waldron was a GP for Tuam sugar factory from the 1930s). Both worked as GPs. My father was also a horse lover and sailor, known across the West. He apportioned a level of notoriety in later life as the breeder of Faugheen, one of Ireland's most revered racehorses. He died driving home, tired and fatigued, from a point-to-point in June 2016. Almost a year after the accident, I found Oscar living alone on a farm, not unlike our own. A black and white long-haired sheepdog estimated to be between two and four years old, Oscar had made a home for himself in a shed on an old, derelict farm near the village of Kilkishen in East Clare.

My father was gregarious and popular. Friends and neighbours marched through the halls of the funeral home, as is traditional in Ireland, for nearly five hours. My hands were covered in blisters afterwards from shaking hands. In the weeks that followed the funeral, I entered something akin to a dream state, compelled by the duties of a son to oversee the various obligations needed to sort out an estate. Numbed from the loss, my body was pent up with get-it-done adrenaline. I met with friends and family and tried to put form to chaos. He had died without a will. This meant a level of stress all around exceeded the usual chaos that sudden death brings. I loved my father, but our relationship was strained, leading up to his death. He had watched his own father die a slow death, and it haunted him. Like W.B. Yeats, the poet laureate of the West of Ireland, he found ageing to be a distressing experience. That he died without pain was a strange comfort, as well as the fact that he had lived on his terms and had a plan to cycle around Jordan before he died. Christmas in 2016 is when grief began in earnest. Although not traditional and no fan of religious ceremony, the symbolic nature of Christmas, when families rally together from all around the globe, brought the loss home like nothing before. I sat at my computer on Christmas Eve playing the song 'Waves' sung by Chance the Rapper on Kanye West's *The Life of Pablo* on repeat, sipping on oversized shots of whiskey. 'Sun don't shine in the shade, birds can't fly in a cage,' the lyrics to the song go, before the line that punched me in the gut, 'Even when somebody go away, the feelings don't....' That year I developed a strange affinity with the song's contradictory sentiment, identifying the trauma of loss as underpinning the album. The sublime beauty of 'Waves' is undeniable, an understanding of grief that rolls in as a series. Some waves are predictable, but others turn tidal.

Sudden death precedes strange, complicated grief. And it is often at its most intense when the noise of daily life is turned down, and friends and colleagues assume the worst has passed. Shock wears thin. In the spring of 2017, as a distraction from the coming anniversary of my father's death, I phoned a friend to let him know I was on the lookout for a dog. Loe, a settled Irish traveler, had kept horses and greyhounds at my father's farm for many years. He had stepped up to the mark after Dad died by keeping everything ticking over on the farm, overseeing its running for two years. I phoned him on a May afternoon to talk about our new home in the country, located in a village called Murroe that we had purchased on the back of the turmoil the previous June. Having witnessed Loe's care of animals firsthand, I knew him to be what many call an animal lover. I trusted his judgment on farm related matters.

Our conversation was short, sweet and to the point:

'Hi Loe'

'Well, Dara.'

'Listen. I want to ask you something.'

'Yea. Go on.'

'I'm getting a dog.'

A SHEEPDOG NAMED OSCAR

'Okay.'

'I'm wondering what dog to get. You've seen where we live when you dropped down the table.'

'Are you beside a farm?'

'Yea. Near a village. There's a dairy farm across from us.'

'Is it fenced off?'

'I suppose it is. There's just a big field behind us.'

'Get a sheepdog Dara. Border collie. They're loyal, they herd. A terrier could chase sheep or cattle and be shot.'

'A working sheepdog?'

'A retired one. Yea.'

'Where will I get one of those?'

'I'll have a look out for one if you want?'

'Ah. Good.'

A sheepdog? A working dog. The type so often seen in rural Ireland tied to a shed by string. The kind of dog that pops up on the old TV series *One Man and His Dog*, running at the beck of a farmer's call? A border collie? I rarely used the name. Where did the name come from? Where was the border in the name? Anything apportioning a border carried negative connotations during the Troubles in Ireland. I therefore adjudged the border to be between Ireland and

Northern Ireland. Then I thought of Wales and England. Finally, I settled on the Scottish and English border. Yep, that's it. My thoughts focused on negative connotations the word 'sheepdog' had when growing up in Ireland. Sheepdogs, back then, were markers of paralysis, a family stuck in time. They signified an unhealthy attachment to the past. They were an impediment to the future. A new world was forming in towns like Tuam as part of the newly emerging post-industrial age. Sheepdogs were signs of an agricultural age with an unwanted influence on the present. Fox-like in appearance, staring up from a crouched position, they roam outside, ready to work at the sound of a farmer's whistle. They stare up with beady eyes, consumed by boundless reservoirs of energy.

As a film researcher by profession, I began to undertake research into sheepdogs and collies online and across media. Border collies are usually, if not always, working dogs: herders. For Irish farmers, a working dog herds sheep and cattle. If it fails to display a required instinct or intelligence, it does not really matter what name is given. A sheepdog is foremost known for an ability to work. One can source a collie from a breeder, I grasped, but if it fails to display a herding instinct (believed it should) it might not even be called a 'sheepdog.' It seemed to me that the terms were really messy, the distinctions between — so important to rural traditions — incredibly hazy.

More information from our initial conversation accrued. I thought it important to follow Loe's advice. All I knew was that I wanted to find some kind of sheepdog, a border collie, whatever that meant. But I had no idea where to look. About to type 'retired border collie/sheepdog' in search engines and social media sites, something serendipitous occurred, a coincidence that came to define a moment of discovery. My job as a university lecturer involves meetings with students on a one-on-one basis. One afternoon in a tutorial with an MA student, a woman by the name of Anne Stewart — when the issue of dog rescue was present on my mind — I took the liberty to interrupt the conversation to ask Anne if she happened to be a dog owner. Anne, originally from Northern Ireland (displaced from Belfast at the age of 13) now lives in Kilkishen, a small village in East Clare. She has been resident in the vicinity for thirty years. Forced to move south during the Troubles, she is still very Northern in her affections. Her eyes lit up when she heard the word 'sheepdog'.

She had seven dogs. Six were Maltese terriers, one a border collie. Her designer son, Michael, sourced the terriers for their luxurious coat, and Anne, a generous animal lover, did not have the heart to sell off all the puppies when they bred. Jake, her trusted collie, was an outside dog and more of a loner than her other batch. Anne described how the pack grew to this number over time. Her home was devoted to the wellbeing of nonhuman animals as well as the human. I mentioned our family's move to the border region between Limerick and Tipperary, indicating my desire to adopt a retiree sheepdog from some place or other. Anne sat back in her chair. Rays of sun pushed through the window, dust particles drifted in the air like granules of a new and coming time. Everything seemed to slow down in that same instant (as I waited for her words with bated breath).

'That's kind of crazy,' a comment wistfully returned in a typically Northern brogue, her dimples pushing against a steely smile. 'There's a wee sheepdog alone on a farm down the road from me. A beautiful thing.'

Wheels of chance began clicking into gear; luck pressing down from some undefined source. It seemed like a ridiculous proposition.

'Nobody owns him?' crept tentatively from my lips.

'No,' Anne replied with some care. 'He strayed to the village and then returned to the farm alone. He's from a farm for sure as he has no collar and stays in a shed.'

I took the time to dwell on her description. 'You mean a stray sheepdog is living there? Who feeds him? Who looks after him by day?'

Anne shifted in her chair; a movement that brought with it a certain unease about the sheepdog's origins. Her tone changed, secreting an air of Northern suspicion. It was a disposition I would gain a greater understanding of as the year progressed. She was tetchy, anxious in her deliberation. She began to sigh, pushing her hair over her eyes in a full swoop.

Then, turning her gaze upon me she declared, 'Collies, two-a-penny, Dara. If the warden gets him, he'll put him down. There are so many across the country. Smart and beautiful animals. The problem is that nobody wants them.'

A SHEEPDOG NAMED OSCAR

'Nobody wants them' was commensurate with an impression formed in childhood. Sheepdogs were remnants of a past to break free from. A picture formed in my mind of a father returning from work with a black and white puppy under arm, a gift from a local farmer. I imagine his children reacting with disdain. Not a sheepdog, not a farm dog: look at how it moves. The children wanted a Labrador or King Charles. A border collie, a common Irish dog, was a fixed entity, stuck in the jaws of time. To come upon the breed in any shape or form was to reject the future. And in the West of Ireland, the future is all we had to cling to. At my desk that afternoon, as the word 'collie' was mentioned again and again, something began to stir. I would kick against the pricks; step out of my inertia. It was mere days since I had spoken to Loe, and now Anne was telling me of a sheepdog that made its way into her life, and possibly mine. A strange redux of excitement and fear washed over me. But it was followed in the aftermath by an urge to ditch the plan for an easier dog.

Why the angst? Hesitancy? I was, of course, warned about the energy levels of collies. I was also concerned that the dog would be in my face day in, day out. I was grieving and didn't need a hyperactive dog in my life. I sat back, listening, before committing to go to see the dog if sent a picture but offering nothing else definite for the time being. I was noncommittal for other reasons: my father's first anniversary lay on the calendar horizon. I lacked the mental and physical fortitude to adopt a dog in the interim weeks. The term 'rescue dog' also

DARA WALDRON

A SHEEPDOG NAMED OSCAR

frightened me; rescue seemed to involve care and attention I wasn't capable of offering. What would happen if the dog was mentally scarred from neglect? What would happen if the dog had developed behavioural issues because of the same? Surely, I wouldn't be able to adopt if that was the case? But I had a stubborn streak, and I had put myself in a position to take it in by asking Anne about dogs, and something had made me want to follow through. At worst, I would get to spend time, having lived far too long in the suburbs, in the countryside. And perhaps, beyond these concerns, things would be okay.

Anne sent the picture to me at the weekend: a digital photograph of a dog staring out from a decrepit shed. It was difficult to read anything definitive into the photograph, other than that the dog had the good sense to find a quiet corner and just stay there. Apparently, the neighbours took to feeding the dog in the evening, yet he still didn't wander down towards their house as a result. He just stayed put. The one person he encountered most — apart from the neighbours — was the farmer's nephew, who was working on the land by day. The farm was left to him by his uncle when he went into a home with dementia. It was an intriguing photograph in that it suggested intelligence and instinct: intelligence to hide in a shed and instinct to find a quiet space on a farm.

There was still much the photograph did not reveal; most of all a personality. Huddling together around a smartphone, enlarging and minimizing the photograph, we attempted to elicit some meaning from the image. My wife and I tried to make sense of pixels ushering only silence. The more we looked at the image, concocting before and after, the more frustrating the gaps in our knowledge became. There were so many questions. How big is he? How dirty? All that was evident in the picture was a head nudging through a door. How feral is he? He sleeps outside in a shed. Is he aggressive? Perhaps he was beaten and is damaged? Anne was heading off for a few days, and although the photo was sent on a Saturday, it wasn't possible to visit the dog — called 'Oscar' — until Wednesday. In the interim, I read up about adopting dogs as a new norm in keeping pets, about alternatives between buying a dog and adopting. So much has changed since my teenage days, so many animals had become unwanted pets. Consumerism had entered the scene. As a result, hundreds of unwanted dogs — once the thrill had passed away — were put up for grabs.

    I began to research animal rescue and the culture around it. Dog ownership has changed so much (in legal terms) in a short space of time. Activists believe it is a moral duty to rescue dogs from abusive owners. Some believe it unethical to breed dogs in a world with so many discarded. Animal rescuers, it appeared, support adoption over buying. Yet, I had not bought a pet in years. I had no idea of the demands for buying. Dog rescuers such as Niall Harbison spend hours with one animal, gently building trust. Activists give services to shelters, donating food and walking dogs. There are so many animal lovers who donate some salary to shelters to keep up their good work. The culture of dog rescue and its focused care has evolved in tandem with an animal rights movement I had some knowledge of from my university years. Animal rights, I understood, are inextricably linked to morals concerning sentient life. Do animals feel emotions and pain like humans? If the answer is yes, to hurt a dog is not so different from abusing a human: some kind of intervention is needed to reintegrate an animal into the folds of regular life. Harbison, who is Irish, has become something of an online sensation in his quest to save as many Thai street dogs as possible, linking the urge to rescue to his recovery from his own self-destructive addictive tendencies. His posts are evidence of the transformative moral purpose around the human urge to rescue fellow animal beings.

The dog peeking out from inside a farmhouse shed — the substance of the photograph Anne sent — had a certain mystique in this regard. The act of peering out from a doorway was near human as an affectation. The photograph seemed to say, 'I'm safe, away from the cruelty of the village, where abuse was hurled in my direction.' There was a gentle configuration to the face of the animal clinging to the security of his shed. Beside the outwards looking eyes was an empty agricultural feedbag along with the frame of an old bed: traces of a forgotten century, signifiers of the past. The animal feed was emblematic of farm life, the bed a family heirloom. What had become, I thought, of the people once attached to these things?

No amount of staring, however, could instill enough confidence to think I had the nurturing capabilities to help a traumatised dog. No amount of speculation could account for a lack of experience; that gnawing feeling I, we, weren't ready to care for the dog. I told Anne I was having second thoughts; my commitment to the idea was waning. In her melodic Belfast whistle, she set me at ease. 'He's a lovely wee thing, Dara, wait and see,' she said, instilling enough confidence in me to allay my creeping concerns.

There were still days to pass. Keeping busy helped quell the doubts harboured about taking the dog home. Work kept creeping uncertainty at bay. On the day to travel out to Kilkishen to finally meet Oscar, the sun burst through the clouds. A long winter had given way to a tentative spring finally offering a blushful summer, manifesting in one of those impenetrably hot days that makes Ireland such a unique place. Moods brighten; people drink in public, and playgrounds fill up; the public — like flowers — blooms instantaneously. We had decided that my then thirteen-year-old son Anton would accompany me and that we would report back to Karl, our younger son, and my wife Ylva when we got home. It was one of those sun-drenched summer evenings that seems designed for lounging about in the countryside, a time to be outside, on an island so often marked by belligerent weather and rain that powers in from an unruly Atlantic.

We ate hastily as the conversation turned to collective excitement. We were consumed with the idea of visiting the farm. The plan was to travel the motorway between Limerick and Clare before hitting the country road. An intense sun shone down. Wind pushed through a half open window, and a cacophony of sound whistled through the air. I searched around for music to quell the lull in adolescent-father relations. Bob Dylan's *Blood on the Tracks* (a favourite) jumped up. 'Tangled Up in Blue' began ringing out as the car lurched forward into an Atlantic headwind. Travelling by motorway to the farm brought with it a clear goal: to rescue a dog and bring him home. It felt good. Life was simple for a change. We had a clarity of purpose. The single by-road to Kilkishen required a left turn from the motorway, taken in the direction of Six Mile Bridge, signaling a change in landscape. A dusty back road replaced the homogeneous concrete of the motorway. Twists and turns released chiaroscuro shadows on overhanging greenery. Bustles of green growth drooped over the front of the ditches like curls on the forehead of a disheveled youth. Anne had planned to meet us in the town of Six Mile Bridge, the idea being that we would tail out with her by car along another back road to the farmyard where Oscar had made his home. She messaged me to say she was running late, so we retreated to the riverside to drink a coke and listen to the draw of the river drifting past. A wild, near romantic mysteriousness seemed to emanate from the ever-changing colour of the water as it trickled down, blue morphing into twisted variations of green and silver.

Folklore and myth have a big role to play in this part of

Clare. It is a region of the island marked by Pagan and early Christian lore. Time is layered in a landscape consisting of wells, ringforts, castles, mountains, and lakes. Lough Derg, one of Ireland's largest, most beautiful lakes, is a key attraction but the region is also scattered with smaller lakes like the one found outside Kilkishen. The former High King of Ireland, Brian Boru, was born near Killaloe and one of his brothers worked as a bishop there. Holy Island on Lough Derg, where relics of early Christian Ireland are preserved and meditative retreats are held year-round, is one of the main attractions.

From the Cromwellian invasion of the 17th century to the Catholic Emancipation movement of the 19th, history erupts from a landscape removed from the otherworldly veneer of the Western seaboard. Hills and musky lakes contrast an austere sea-beaten landscape of the Burren (particularly in summer) in the West of the county. As you approach Kilkishen it is like an arrow of time inches you forward in increments; the driver suspended in a terrain of rusting signs and church spires reaching to the sky. It is like one is breathing in and out of time's gills. We tracked Anne's car along a by-road, passing by the playpark and fields of grazing cattle on a steep incline, at which point a smaller by-road folded in upon us. It was like moving back through centuries, back through to a time when horses and traps were the main source of transport across the island. Back to a time when the first experiments in communism were being held in the

Ralahine area, long before communism came to fruition. The commune of Ralahine founded near Newmarket-on-Fergus in 1831 was a radical resistance to colonial-religious hierarchy, an inspiration for The Ralahine Center for Utopian Studies at University of Limerick, of which I am an affiliate member.

The car pulled in at Anne's cottage, on a slight bend in the road. In the valley below, a small turlough glistened against a radiant sky. At the roadside cottage, the spectacular view from the estate made itself known, like a magical impression of a lost Bruegel masterpiece. Symmetrical hills shouldered a bespoke lake, along which several small boats sailed upon the surface. To the right of this was a steeper incline; the fields peppered with buttercups and medium-sized bushes of gorse. Sheep and newly born lambs decorated the hills with their greater expanse of green. A two-story house, beside which was a farm, was seated further down the road.

We had arrived at the cottage, a small and cute abode with a shed and partly manicured garden, set out beside a bend in the road. Stepping from the car, a sudden influx of colour appeared.

'Where is Oscar camped?' I asked, Anton fidgeting beside me.

Adjusting her rimmed spectacles, Anne pointed at the hills across from us. The farm could be got at from two directions, she announced, a frontward looking gap in the wall where visitors enter, and a back requiring a short trek up a steep hill.

'Nice here,' I said, restless but keen at the same time.

With a collar and leash we took off for the back entrance; trekking up a trail that would lead to the shed Oscar made his home. Because the terrain was hilly it was difficult for Anne to maneuver. We decided to change route to one of the lesser inclined steps of land, before calling on a neighbour (a veterinary nurse who was feeding Oscar) to say hello and then walking along the man-made path back to the entrance of the farm.

It is difficult — not impossible — to describe the breathtaking beauty at the top of the hill before entering the walled garden where, once inside, Oscar was waiting. The shed, as shown in the photograph that Anne had sent on, was hidden in this space. We passed through an inlet, over cowpats, to the gate of a stunning 18th-century walled garden. With a curved design (so unlike the strict line so popular today), the space yielded its own resolute beauty.

'He's in here,' Anne said to me, with some trepidation. She so wanted me to take him home.

But I was getting ready to back pedal, fashion a way out of taking the dog. Now firmly inside the farm, on the cobblestone path that lay beneath a shaky red gate, it seemed like we broke through a bubble of time, settling in a different century. There was something entirely magical about the quasi-symmetrical curvature of stone around; a space where animals could move freely within the enclosure. To the right of this, through the gate, was the stately home marked by a caved-in roof. It was, Anne said, a listed building protected by the state. Everything around the house was born of ancient longevity. It was a world encased with the timeless serenity of stone.

'Anne, what's the story with the collapsed roof?' I asked, before the moment ceded — like the sky had fallen in and the ground was littered with clouds — to a black and white spurt. My eyes adjusted to an image slowly making its form apparent: a sheepdog. The dog's tail was moving back and forward at such a rate it was nearly banging his head against itself repetitively. It was a full-body shuffle more than a straightforward tail wag. I hunched down, brushing my hand against the matted clots in his coat to rub the dog's stomach. The dog's tentative stare out from the shed in the picture had gripped my attention, but now he was looking at me in a completely unexpected fashion: this dog who was so infused with the joy of life. Since Anne mentioned 'stray' and 'rescue' in the office, my mind had been consumed with images of a disgruntled dog, in fear of human contact and in need of care. But I still needed caution to offset an image that braced my attention as a child: that of an angry growling dog afraid of every move, an animal terrorized by fear. Suddenly, against these feisty imaginations, was the friendliest dog I ever set eyes on.

Oscar was jumping on his back legs before lying down again, placing the side of his face against the ground — a pose I later read is a typical collie mannerism — his tail wagging and eyes staring with intent. He rubbed his face along the ground

DARA WALDRON

The abandoned farm near Kilkishen where Oscar was living.
Wrapped silage to feed livestock seen in the foreground.

A SHEEPDOG NAMED OSCAR

before jumping up again. My first impression, that the dog who was living in the shed would need to be coaxed out with canine treats, was shattered with his electric movement; he was so enamoured with contact, so taken with humans. His introduction was overwhelming. We fed him treats on the cobblestone, sausages in foil, which he ate slowly, and examined the shed he had made his home. A little battered bowl, half-filled with multi-colored kibble, stood out against a concrete floor aligned with discarded farm materials. Weeds had begun shooting up from cracks in the concrete like nature reclaiming the space for itself. The farm seemed to have lost its way, to have stopped battling the ageing imprint of years that had passed.

The growth stood out the most on this shrouded estate: Nature's attempts to reclaim land over time. The house was a formative trace of the British ascendancy's determining presence in Ireland. First built in 1846, years before falling into the hands of a descendent bachelor farmer I was told was in the throes of dementia, it was originally registered as the estate of Henry Thomas Baylee. The estate was too big a repair for the owner, an irony given a Baylee daughter married Percy le Clerc, a leading architect known countrywide for restoring property. Holycross Abbey and Bunratty Castle form part of his extended portfolio.

The sheepdog at my feet had made it to a corner of rural Ireland, touched by the once dominant classes on the island. It was a world that still existed on the margins of everyday life. The walled-in oasis was in a sea of ancient and mythical beauty; a site where British Colonialism reached early Christian and Pagan Ireland, mixing with everything else in-between. Peering across the landscape, the lake sparkling against a turning light, cottages sat quietly on the hills peppered with freshly grown grass and buttercups, seductive cues for the wandering eye. A ruined castle of sorts lay dormant on the horizon, across which was a row of bungalow bliss cottages, the light falling on the houses forming a bristle of shadows and silhouettes. A hazy wind blew across the field, gusting along the lake, bleating sheep in a pastoral haven, calling out like sirens to the oncoming, distant night.

How did Oscar get here? What had brought him to an abandoned farm? Anne relayed the story about the farmer's debilitating dementia, the estate advancing into disrepair. Yet, this was Oscar's shed, his secure and safe space. Perhaps it really was his home? Maybe he really was the farmer's dog? It was a farm, after all, in one of the biggest sheep farming regions: a site embedded with agricultural tradition. As I looked all around the space, Anton was fidgeting; consumed by Oscar's powers of exertion, both of us struggling to get our bearings. I said we would take him. There was nothing more to do, other than to bring him home as part of the family. Work commitments meant stalling for a few days, until Sunday that weekend, to collect him from the farm, perhaps compromising safety. But just as we were about to return to the car, he began to follow in the same direction.

DARA WALDRON

A SHEEPDOG NAMED OSCAR

At that moment I felt the urge to bring him with us. It was an all-encompassing desire.

Instead, I said 'stay' repeatedly. He turned and hunkered at the gate, eyeballing me with a guilty stare. My urge to care for him, to shelter him from the threat of the wild surfaces beyond the farmyard walls, was suddenly overbearing. It was hard to push back the image of his face between the steel gate, whimpering like a child who misses his mother. In the years that followed that first visit to the farm, I often look back and berate myself for leaving him in the savagery of a world impervious to his goodness. But I had not planned to keep him then, and the necessary bits to bring him home were not in place. There were no supplies to nurture him. I thought it best not to disturb Oscar any more than was necessary at that given moment. But when we got back to the car, thinking that the land had called out to us, it suddenly felt like the visit returned a resounding 'Yes!!'

The light had yet to dim on the drive over county lines as night was emerging, a warm wind gusting in the window, confirming summer's arrival. Ylva was at the stairs when we got home, coaxing Karl to sleep. It was almost dark as we sprinted, pushing into a quiet room to report on the evening.

'It's strange,' I said, 'it feels like he was dropped on my lap from above.' I've never met an animal that is so infused with life. It's hard to believe he's a stray, abandoned or whatever happened to him.'

Then Anton responded, 'You should have heard him

whimpering as we were leaving. He lay on his stomach and cried like he had known us forever.' My wife smiled while nodding in confirmation. An air of excitement began to fill the room. The rest of the week would be taken up sourcing provisions for a dog, preparing for Oscar the sheepdog to arrive home.

The local pet shop yielded the basics: kibble and a bowl to eat and drink from, a sleeping basket; a collar and a lead to gentrify. Our house sits beside Glenstal Abbey, a former Ascendency estate home to a Benedictine Order on the edge of Murroe. The house itself is located around the corner from the front gates to the monastery. Our initial plan was to walk Oscar through the grounds of the estate. He would need, however, to look like a respectable pet to do so, capable of walking on a leash. I stocked up on doggie treats to begin the lessons in recall, thinking of a time when walking the trails, he would instantly return to me through call alone. First, however, the do's and don'ts had to be checked off one by one; the things to keep a pet in check. I rang Anne on Saturday to let her know we would be coming the next day. Anne offered to collect Oscar from the farm, meaning we were able to pick him up from her place on the Sunday evening. It made it all so much easier.

On Sunday at Anne's house, two cars were needed to transport several family members. Ylva went with Anton and my Mum, who was visiting for the weekend. Karl and I travelled in another car. On the second journey to Kilkishen (with the ruins of Kilkishen Castle standing up like a gift from the Gods), *Blood on the Tracks* played on the stereo for the second time. I mentioned that I sang 'I can't help it if I'm lucky' from 'Idiot Wind' — one of the most iconic songs on what many believe to be Dylan's best album — to his Mum when we started dating. I explained the importance of the song to the origin of our family. We were on our way to an old countryside farm together — to rescue a sheepdog. Life was straightforward for once. Everything was concentrated on a simple act, a collective family occasion. The silhouette of Bunratty Castle could be glimpsed from the road to the 'Bridge, and as 'Shelter from the Storm' played again, a lone tear crept down my cheek.

'Shelter from the Storm' is one of the most cherished Dylan songs. It consists of a three-chord progression played on an acoustic guitar, over which the song verse rings out. It is generally accepted that *Blood on the Tracks* is one of the greatest singer-songwriter albums in history, an album concerning the tumultuous breakdown of Dylan's marriage to his wife, Sara. 'Shelter from the Storm' reads like one long lyrical struggle. An everyman figure, looking for shelter from a raging storm, takes refuge from a woman. In one sense, an allegory surrounding Dylan's personal struggles at the time, it is also something else: a furtive insight into the depths of the human condition. The image of a woman offering care to a weather-beaten man, during an environmental storm that doubles as emotional, taps into the human instinct to care.

'In a world of steel-eyed death, and men who are fighting to be warm,' Dylan sings, inviting the refrain, 'come in she said I'll give you shelter from the storm.' The car pushed headlong into the wind, the magnetic sun drawing the family towards clouds sat upon mountains, the song reaching into the depths of my gut. I imagined a poor decrepit animal, beaten and abandoned, banished from the village. And then I thought of the photograph Anne had sent: Oscar peering out through a shed doorway. Was I the woman in Dylan's 'Shelter;' a carer of forsaken souls in the midst of a ravaged earth?

Dylan's song played over again, with each line nudging me closer to the idea that to care for a dog could somehow become a panacea for the physical shock consuming me that year. Three weeks after driving to see Oscar for the first time I stood at the back of a church marking my father's anniversary. Grief had come in unexpected moments, incisions interrupting the struggle to understand. That struggle would lessen in time, of course. But on the drive to the country to collect a sheepdog from a farm, a singular desire was pushing through; to return life to the world. Our intentions were centered on a sharpening will in the pull of desire— the solace to be found deep in the soul of the countryside. To shelter this rapacious bundle of joy would soon become my calling.

The line from the song 'a place where it's always safe and warm' spilled out into the breeze, pushing through a window like a cushion of unfiltered affection. My storm was sudden death: clouds that descend in an instant. A farm, horses, a dog, a cat: an estate only the deceased knew how to run; a son who knew little about the intricacies of farming life; a scatter of hangers-on claiming to be his close friends. How to know, how to distinguish? How to find shelter? And beyond the practicalities of death were questions that would not relent: where are you? Where did you go? In a storm of unanswered questions, I glanced over at the child in the passenger seat, a boy learning to comprehend the world, when a shared purpose seemed to come from above — to covet life in a storm of complicated emotions that had descended for those driving to collect a dog.

The two cars moved in convoy, pushing into wind, past gorse, overladen hedges, elements of nature soon to be in bloom. The hills of Clare, meshed in summer color, returned my thinking to Bruegel's masterpiece *Hunters in the Snow*. For years I had been preoccupied with the meaning of the winter scene — the pictorial cautioning against a powerful ability to affect. In the painting, peaks and valleys roll under a carpet of winter, hills that hold the hunters giving way to a valley, beyond which gangs of children are seen skating on ice. The perspective is a key to understanding the scene: the hunters are mere silhouettes monitored from behind, the spectacular snow-covered hills devoid of animal life. Dogs accompany the hunters, one of whom carries a dead fox on his back, all of them staring at the snow, hunching down in forward motion, demoralized by the cold. Barren trees; a single crow, a symbol of death, hovering overhead; a woman

DARA WALDRON

Pieter Bruegel the Elder, *Hunters in the Snow* (1565)
Kunsthistorisches Museum, Vienna

flaying a pig, a tradition associated with peasant-life in the Netherlands. Below, in the distant valley, peasants wait on hunters tasked with scavenging for food in times of scarcity amidst the ravages of winter. In the picture's composition the scene foregrounds hunters. But the peasants whose leisure relies on their pursuits are far away in the distance, the landscape engulfs them: the once-fertile valley to work in warmer months.

As a professor of cinema, the painting holds special meaning. I began my doctoral studies exploring the moral treatment of evil by filmmakers, consumed by the films of Pier Paolo Pasolini and Robert Bresson. Over time, I was drawn more to landscape and the way emotions are invested in the earth as part of broader ethnographic pursuits. I began exploring these issues in films like *sleep furiously* (2008), a faux documentary about a small village in Mid-West Wales. I found Gideon Koppel's film, although not explicitly about the filmmaker's mother, to be movingly so. The land is a key character in a film that fleshes out the connection formed with weather and changing seasons. Russian filmmaker Andrei Tarkovsky hung a print of *Hunters in the Snow* on the Soviet spaceship in his sci-fi masterpiece *Solaris* to emphasize this very point. In his later auto-fictional film *Mirror* — my all-time favourite — the painting's depiction of hills and valleys comes to life as a scene from Tarkovsky's childhood during the war. As we drove to Kilkishen that second evening, the painting's auratic meaning seemed to reach out to me anew. Imagining the disgruntled hunters returning from the hunt seemed to mirror my own journey that calendar year. I too became a hunter searching, looking for existential truth — where does the soul go when the body dies? It seemed a heavy storm of melancholic maladjustment: the weight of grief is to look and not find.

I fiddled around with the stereo, so that 'Shelter for the Storm' played on repeat. Thoughts of Dylan and Bruegel synced as if designed to fall together. Karl nonchalantly gazed out the window, fixated on traces of Ylva and others moving in the distance. I stopped the car at a ditch, a by-road, before taking another to Anne's house for the second time that week. As a murmuration of starlings fluttered across a field of clad stone surfaces in which a ruined cottage sat in one corner of the field, a group of cattle in the other, a light brown coloured cow mulching on grass peered in my direction. I winked back, opening the door to stretch my legs. A motionless landscape greeted me like a screen of discarded objects. My eyes tripped over wild stumps of grass growing out from stone wall crevices before a quick breath and a swing around to the front of the car got me moving away again. Once the car ignition triggered and the lights came on, the music began to play again. This time however, instead of ushering me into the world of *Hunters in the Snow*, I awoke to a different season. No longer ensconced in winter's snow, a glaring sun reached out towards me.

We were at a junction before taking the road to where

A SHEEPDOG NAMED OSCAR

Oscar was waiting. A field to our left was littered with haystacks, a rare sight in the Irish landscape, given the changes to agriculture in decades past. They are replaced — en masse — with synthetic parcels of silage produced by machines. On sight of the first, a later Bruegel painting, *The Harvesters*, came to mind, a homage to summer. Unlike the silhouettes in *Hunters in the Snow*, faces hidden, *The Harvesters* depicted on wood panels are a much bigger scale, more easily discerned by the viewer. Our car began to slow to a snail's pace as I peered over at the haystacks standing like sculptures made specifically for the field. I imagined the fields populated by families, communities coming together to make the winter manageable for animals and humans alike. My mind turned upon a network of memories: summer days spent turning turf, long afternoons labouring; Indian summers spent deep in the throes of labour. Then I thought of the vital activities purporting to be of the Irish landscape that had died with the onset of the industrial and information age. It was all beginning to take shape, crystallizing around a sheepdog we were about to collect. We were en route to rescue a sheepdog named Oscar. It felt right. The year was fresh with purpose — to safeguard a sheepdog from the perils of the world.

Like *Hunters in the Snow*, *The Harvesters* is a painting that encourages the gaze of the beholder to wander from a height, a point where peasants are resting from the summer sun to a place where hay is harvested. The gaze moves along the horizon line. It moves to the valleys, where children play

DARA WALDRON

Pieter Bruegel the Elder, *The Harvesters* (1565)
Metropolitan Museum of Art, New York

in parks. Beyond the harvest is the sea, the ships like dots on a mystical expanse of ocean. Unlike the real Netherlands, Bruegel's landscape is an imaginary place of deep peaks and valleys.

The Harvesters is a homage to labour: the land. Years of suburban dwelling severed my link to the land. I came to the painting in its pictorial simplicity as an invocation of days growing up in rural Ireland; evenings spent throwing bales of hay to passing trucks: jokes, the thirst, the feeling of working on something greater than the individual — the earth. Anne's cottage overlooked a Bruegel-like lake. Once its outline appeared, my memory of evenings spent waiting for the go ahead to hit the town ignited — the end of harvest with its sensations intact: a smell in the air, gush of pollinated flowers, a hazy breeze when sunburn fizzled against reddened cheeks. Our convoy was about to arrive at her cottage just as Anne came out smiling to greet us. My mother opened a door and happily made her way to Anne. And then two more doors opened in a moment of synchronicity. Ylva and the two boys stepped away from the car in anticipation of the change that lay ahead.

I removed the collar and leash from the glove compartment, turned my gaze over my shoulder to see Karl standing tentatively away from the car. Our reckoning had come. Oscar would return with us. Mum and Anne were deep in conversation beside the front gate just off the road and Ylva was waving over to Karl and me. Along the path, hedges ringed the surrounding heather in harmony, with the yellow-infused gorse standing out like dabs of paint on stretched canvas. A more than significant odour of cattle manure filtered through the air and the sound of machinery in the distant fields echoed over. The area was a hive of unfettered nature. I strolled over to Anne and Ylva, my mother and the two boys, to wait excitedly, along with the others, for the big moment to arrive.

'I'll go to get him,' Anne said, as we nodded back in agreement. 'Just try not to overwhelm him,' she added, before turning her back to us. Then she took off to the side of her cottage. Thirty seconds later, she returned with a ragged sheepdog in tow.

Oscar was pulling hard on the leash, dragging Anne along with him. He was so low to the ground it was difficult to recognize the contours of a particular species. Then he began to assess the space around him, in a frenzy of excitement, unnerving my mother so much she retreated to the car. His tail was moving so quickly it was banging against his head again, leading us to form a small circle around him. Away from the farmyard Oscar's tangled mat was another part of an unexpectedly disheveled appearance; his demeanour that of an abandoned animal cast adrift in a world to fend for himself. I stood back, looking over his body with some discomfort, my earlier unease returning with renewed vigour. 'We'll have to get him into the car, Anne,' I said, before Ylva instantly replied, 'I'll hold him.' Failure, on my part, to adequately respond haunted me for a long time after — I didn't trust my instinct to hold Oscar in my arms. Why was I afraid? Why was I holding back, allowing others to do the job? The truth is I was fearful, haunted by an advert from national TV as a child. In the advert, a rabies-infested dog is cornered. When a hand is shown reaching to comfort the dog, the creature bares its teeth aggressively, before building into a full-blooded attack. The advert was meant to encourage dog owners to get their dogs vaccinated. But for me it was an exposure to animal violence that stayed with me long after. Instead of holding Oscar in the car to let him know he was safe — allowing Ylva to drive — I took refuge in the driver's seat.

'Some dogs don't like to be lifted,' Anne muttered while I stared at one cowering in fear, before swinging the door open and dangling a piece of 'deer meat' seductively in front of him.

'Think he's never been in a car?' I said to Anne when confronted for the first time with the size of the task. Maybe Oscar was a feral of sorts?

'Probably not,' Anne said forcefully, before Ylva rose to the task, allowing me to mask my fear. It was a decision on my wife's part that I think Oscar remembers, such is the affection he has for her to this day; in many ways I think he sees her as his protector.

Ten minutes were taken up bungling a medium-sized, terrified sheepdog into the back of a Toyota. Oscar jumped away at first, sliding his body underneath the rear of the car.

He shivered as I poked at him with a small twig, an attempt to coax him out towards the deer treats; I was trying, throughout, to be as gentle as possible with him.

'Is he afraid?' I asked Anne, appearing confident when I was likely to be the one most afraid.

'No, no,' Anne replied, 'he's been through a really tough few weeks.'

Eventually he was lured out from under using synthetic dog treats. We closed the door hastily to give him enough space to jump into the passenger seat in pursuit of the treat placed on the opposite side of the car to where I was sitting.

'If you let down the front seat and climb in that way, Ylva, we'll get him in,' I said, appearing to be in control of things when it was anything but the case. Then I motioned to Anne to close the door in a big simultaneous push, using both my hands to help push him back in from the side.

Suddenly, he was in.

We had to get on the road as swiftly as possible. Gesturing over at the others to jump in quickly, I called out, 'thanks for everything, I'll be in touch soon' in Anne's direction before Ylva squeezed into the backseat while petting Oscar. A puddle of drool formed on the floor. As soon as the car began to move the drool increased in form and Ylva — having little or no experience of dogs — was unable to stop it. She spoke to Oscar in Swedish, using phrases I hadn't heard since our children were toddlers. (Her shift into Swedish, that first real communication with Oscar, would have a lasting impact; for years I began to practice — unknown to myself — pidgin Swedish with Oscar. It was only when watching videos of us together that I finally realised what I was doing.) The car pushed against the rays of evening sun, arresting us, the landscape stretching out in front, as I inquired about how Oscar was doing in the back seat. And then, just as the car made its way up the driveway to our new house, worries returned with vengeance: What were we taking on? Why had we signed up for this? What state was Oscar really in?

Oscar's head lurched backwards and forwards, as he stared at the floor. Ylva stroked his coat, whispering everything would be okay, he was safe. Not to overcomplicate was one of many admirable qualities. 'Come in, she said, I'll give ya shelter from the storm' pushed into my thoughts, the silhouettes from *Hunters in the Snow* an accompanying visual. I imagined the woman flaying a pig offering sustenance to hunters. Was Oscar getting similar sustenance? From a woman he only met. The return home was a blur, one of those drives when details coalesce into a haze: when experience flows so fast all context evaporates. Once we had ascended the drive home, the mountains appeared aloof in the diminishing light, an odour of recently spread silage from adjacent farms filtering in the window. My mother and the boys were waiting. Anton was holding a lead, ready to show Oscar the expanses of the field adjacent to our house. I stepped out of the car as the door swung open. Oscar jumped out, as the group appeared ready to show him the home wonders.

But the dog that ventured into the yard that evening bore little resemblance to the joyful mess that first appeared on the hillside farmyard a few days earlier. He was subdued, out of kilter. Before I had time to consider why, he had already jumped to make his way underneath the engine. My envisaged strolls in the runaway pastures of home, hand in hand with a domesticated sheepdog beckoning my command, were destroyed in an instant. I used a stick to poke at Oscar to get him out.

'He's probably scared,' I declared, attempting to puncture the disappointment, coax him slowly. 'It's obvious he's never been in a car before,' I said, my mother trying — at the same time — not to irritate in offering advice but managing to irritate me by quizzically asking, 'Are you sure you know what you're doing?' Of course, I had no idea what we were doing. That was why I was leaning underneath the car, poking a stick at Oscar. There was nothing straightforward, no reason for my attempt to lure him from under, which was probably the point of the exercise. Before prodding him with any major intent, Oscar had come out and shuttled over towards the lawn, stretching out in a submissive pose.

'Get the leash on him,' I shouted over to the group, seeing Ylva was hunching down in a squat-like poise, 'quick... before he runs away and into the field.'

A human chain circled around a dog so frightened he shuffled onto the cut lawn within our immediate vicinity, his head bowed down.

A SHEEPDOG NAMED OSCAR

'Why isn't he excited like he was before?' Anton asked inquisitively, to which there was no immediate and obvious answer. I googled 'rescue dog comes home for first time. What next?' on my phone. By the time answers began flooding in, Ylva had begun to walk Oscar around the garden's tree-heavy boundary, as the group stared in awe. He had no concept of being on a lead and his neck, hemmed in so that he was pulling awkwardly in all directions, jerked him forward. So much of what had seemed normal on the farm — his size and appearance — now matted hair and coat stood out. He looked like anything but a domesticated pet. It was like he had fallen from some wild Godforsaken land. The initial thrill on finding him dissipated. My repressed fears, pushed under my skin, began to surface as undesired responsibilities. It didn't seem like the dog we met before.

But it was, of course, the same dog. It was just the context that changed. At the farm, animals were in direct earshot, the place had a rundown 'farm' feel. It was normal to see an unkempt sheepdog roaming around. Go to any Irish farm, and similarly uncouth working dogs will stare up at you. But the return home changed things. I watched a scared, perhaps traumatised animal walk tentatively around the garden, wondering if I was in the right frame of mind to care for him. My life was rocked. I was struggling to care for myself. I lacked concentration and due diligence to take on the responsibility. That first evening on the farm, the hills were luscious in beauty. We breathed the summer air into our furtive lungs, like we had entered the scene of a Dylan Thomas poem. Life was reaching a pitch of mystical perfection, captivating as an experience. Now, the warning 'a dog is for life' was a missile hitting its target. A part of me had been seduced by the romanticism of it all, enthralled by the splendour of the countryside. The evening lent itself to poetic musings: images of man and nature in symbiosis. Reality intervened. I watched an overwhelmed sheepdog walk around a leylandii-enclosed garden, my mother, wife, and children looking on. It felt too much to take on. Oscar bowed his head, the crusts of mud dangling from his long-haired coat. Clouds began to gather above, and the rain threatened a sudden downpour. The collective began to run for cover. I ran over to help Ylva escort Oscar into the patio room, the 'one bedroom apartment' we had put in place for him that weekend leading to his first big day at home.

Our house, in its present form, took shape in increments, over several decades. The original 1960s build was extended in the '70s, making two points of entry. One looks out at leylandii trees that bookend a path leading out to the field of a local farmer, Frank Ryan. Bay windows open to a view of the Silvermines Mountains from the rear entrance, sheltering the patio room. A little heater sits in the corner of the patio for cold nights, beside which we placed a basket and cushions for a medium-sized dog. The doggie stuff was sourced from a city superstore earlier in the week before considerable time was spent making the patio as appealing for a new guest as possible. Oscar's first and second evenings were subdued. Settled to a degree, he remained devoid of the life force encountered on the farm. My initial concern was that he would bark to get out of the room, waking up our 89-year-old neighbour Michael, who the house was purchased from. Obviously, nobody wanted this to happen. Nobody wanted Oscar to end up in a pound or a rescue center. It was hard to countenance ever having to do something so drastic. But there was serious concern that he would wake Michael up at night. But he never barked for that first week. Nor did he bark the first month or year. That evening, against the flow of catastrophic projections, Oscar remained silent. He slept on the far side of the patio room to where the bed lay and didn't open his mouth to make a sound. He was tired. When peering in, I saw him sprawled out on the bare floor. All the time spent picking a bed, then deciding to go with a hand-woven basket, was of little worth; when the time arrived, Oscar remained impervious to the fact it was his. The next day I rang a friend who volunteers with Animal Welfare. I was looking for some basic advice about dogs' behaviour. Several cues came from our initial chat. First, it was tiring for Oscar. Fatigue overwhelmed him that evening. Second, it was a kind of trauma, brought about when removed from the farm that had become a safe space.

The advice made sense. Instead of a high-energy response to deep stress like the shakeup from fleeing quickly, or a tentative expression of fear, it was first hard to identify the trauma in Oscar because his initial response took the opposite form. My friend pointed out that Oscar was probably never in a car, was unlikely to have been microchipped, and was probably riddled with fleas and worms. He told me to take him to a vet and groomer, to put wheels of nourishment in motion.

On the day of the visit to the groomer, Oscar had to be coaxed into a car with towels and treats, the former to take the hit of constant drooling. It would be my first visit to a dog groomer, a Geordie who was married to an Irish woman and living in proximity to Newport in Tipperary. I had no idea what the groomer did. The Ireland of my youth had little by the way of dog grooming businesses. Indeed, the culture of keeping pets in 21st-century Ireland was new to me. 1980s Ireland was an economic blackspot, families could just about afford to feed a dog, never mind professionally groom them. The pet world had changed beyond all recognition. I got to the groomer with a mere modicum of understanding for the profession. Once John appeared, however, I knew I was in the presence of a dog lover (of German Shepherds in particular). He led Oscar into a garage that was given over to his grooming work. He then set about easing my concerns, stressing that Oscar needed a good combing and washing down. There was nothing about him, he said, to make him think Oscar was abused before he came into our life. John assured me it was an adjustment phase after leaving the farm, a place where he had felt safe and secure. After chatting a little with John, and once the grooming work had begun, I was told to return in about three hours to collect Oscar.

A short distance from John's house, on the Limerick-to-Murroe Road was an accessible riverside walk. Cherry blooms fell into a wet depression that marked a sudden transformation in the landscape. A field of grazing sheep faced a wet marshy bog. I parked, removed a small cushion from the car boot with the plan of sitting in the sun for an hour or two by the river. Setting off with a bag, sunglasses, and a book, I had assumed the grooming time would take an hour or possibly two but never three. In the distance, a farmer was ushering cattle towards a gate, accompanied by a teenage boy I assumed to be his son helping in the process. The cattle appeared to me dabs of colour in the glowing sunshine, the field a moving frame of composition. It was a pastoral scene encountered every day in rural Ireland. As it appeared, the scene triggered the memory of the evening prior to news breaking about my father's accident. We were making our way home from Ballybunion Beach. A farmer appeared in front of me moving cattle from one field to the next, signaling to drivers to slow down. As the car slowed to a standstill, I turned to the kids and joked that we were 'caught in traffic.' The cattle rolled slowly by the window, as I took a moment to glance at my phone. There was a missed call, emblazoned by the word 'Dad.' For a moment I thought of returning it. But it was a long way home from the beach. We were tired and it could wait.

DARA WALDRON

A SHEEPDOG NAMED OSCAR

Weeks passed dwelling on about having not returned the call, that the call might have changed the scheme of events and thus the course of time. The call might have broken the causal chain. The fatal accident leading to my father's passing might have been avoided; one phone call might have made a difference. The call was never made, and time took its course. Maybe, I reasoned, he would call me back. But an hour after getting back home, I was manning a barbecue; sun-scorched kids running circles around me. I never rang back, made *that* call. A year or so had passed, before I sat by the Mulcair, the water lulling my senses, all my attention consumed with questions that would never be answered. Where are you? What happens to the souls of those we love when they die?

There was some time remaining before John finished grooming. The plan was to walk the riverbank for a few hundred yards, as far as the pathway extended to where the current gathered in strength. At a wall that seemed to conclude the riverside path a field was littered with sheep and newborn lambs. There must have been a hundred lambs in a field that was three or four, possibly five acres wide. It was a pastoral haven, a fertile expression of nature set with human hands. Ewes were feeding newborn lambs, and lambs lolled in the grass. The scene cued me to remember a lecture attended as a graduate student at the University of Exeter. A newly appointed professor was giving an inauguration lecture, a tradition for appointments to Chair. She was talking about care, a research area pioneered by feminist Carol Gilligan.

Attendees were packed in a stuffy theatre, massively overheated by human bodies. Beads of sweat trickled down the front of my brow as the professor began to address the crowd about the ethics of 'care.' Care cultivates life as interdependent. Care, the audience were told that day, cultivates the ethical plurality of being. It is an ethics feminists turned to in the '80s to highlight the plural nature of being in its human form.

Feminism, as I understood it back then, was the strategic struggle for equality among the sexes, not a way of caring for another person relationally and ethically. Care as a condition of interdependent beings stayed with me long after as a conceptual concern. Care as a source of love. Ancillary claims that same day were made in tandem with a theory premised on differences of 'emotional' and 'rational' knowledge: males are taken in by abstraction, rights, and justice, contrasting feminine emphasis on nurturing relationships. Males are drawn to logic and reason, the feminine to emotional relations. Gilligan's ethics have since been deemed essentialist, her research seen as reductive around the distinction 'man' and 'woman,' but none of this seemed to impact upon me as I peered at a field. Ewes were caring for lambs, as I waited on a sheepdog.

Over the course of a year, memories like these sifted through in random moments. It would feel like the membrane that is designed to stop emotions overwhelming us, broke in two at inopportune moments in time. Music triggered memories of time spent with my father. U2's album *The Joshua Tree* was a case in point, summoning memories so vivid it was like I could reach out to touch his body from up close. He was there but, of course, he was not. Grief was the name used to describe this experience, when involuntary memories cultivated a desire, never met, to reach out and hold.

The memory of the inaugural address was a cue to think about nourishing care. Taking care would reduce the seeking that consumes grieving. Perhaps, in the throes of the care relationship, a differing source of knowledge would make itself known to me. Where does the line between emotion and reason lie? As I turned away from the field that day to peer into the river and all its translucent water, shades of blue exported an effervescent green. The river sparkled with the blush of an awakening sunshine. Baby trout spun back and forth as nature began to cradle me in its grasp.

Then a trickle of rain pushed through clouds. I realised it was time to collect Oscar. Nestled under a wall — with just enough light to make out the phone screen — I texted John immediately, to make sure it was okay. Minutes later, John replied that Oscar would be ready to leave in half an hour.

Walking the riverbank that afternoon, I began to imagine a newly constructed image of a no-longer-ragged sheepdog. A couple and child advanced in my direction, hand signaling hello. In a rush to return to the vibrant thoughts of care on the sun-laden riverbank, cherry blossoms pushing newly formed petals onto the walkway, I returned a smile in their direction.

I was the woman in 'Shelter in the Storm'; Bruegel's muse calling to the hunters. All I could think about was Oscar.

At John's place the words 'come on in' rang out from the garage. As the door opened Oscar was at a table hemmed in by a metal harness. Clots of hair gathered across a wooden floor. A large beach-coloured German Shepherd slept in a silver crate in the corner of the same room. He woke up to look in my direction, content his master had the dog grooming honours with Oscar instead of him. Oscar's long coat had been transformed. He looked like he had months of good living to his name and was bristling with energy as a result.

'Such a great job you've done, thanks a lot John,' I said, handing him a trivial fee for three hours of intensive grooming work on Oscar. 'No bother at all,' John replied, as he began to speak of his life as a painter and decorator and lifelong love of dogs. He had kept German Shepherds for as long as he could recall, he said, first encountering the breed as a child. His family were breeders and had entered their dogs in competition. As a result, he had been educated from a very early age in the art of dog grooming for show.

John spoke of his life-long battle with the medical condition of osteogenesis: 'brittle bones.' He worked as a painter/decorator all his life, when able to manage his health condition accordingly. Age took its toll and his condition worsened, ending his career. Dog grooming was not just a business, but a way of staying busy around an activity he loved. It was his trust in dogs laid out on his table that had impressed me the most; a trust he invested quickly in a sheepdog who was found living alone on a farm. I questioned him about Oscar, attempting to tap into the wisdom that came from having worked with dogs all his life.

'Is he okay?' I inquired. 'Do you think he has been abused?'

As he shuffled about in his chair a silence accompanied the stooped pose. I waited for the conversation to gather pace as a finger on a thumb was used to signal a soon to be made cup of tea. Gesturing a thumbs up in return, I relocated to the front of the house to put Oscar in the car. John, scuttling to the kitchen, arrived around to the front minutes later with tea and some biscuits. He spoke at length about working dogs, the special temperament of German Shepherds. Although they have been mostly co-opted as pets, he said, the breed has a longstanding working tradition: search and rescue dogs and even herding. Like collies, he mentioned, winking at Oscar in the car, they are extremely intelligent. It was the first but not the last time that I would hear 'intelligence' used to describe the mentality of a dog. It was interesting — no doubt — but as a discussion point, I didn't find it particularly useful (we think of human intelligence, which cannot be the same).

Two points of emphasis made by John to me that day lingered long after: submissiveness and companionship. In response to my query about abuse, he said Oscar is very submissive. Some submissive dogs have been treated badly. It is not always the case that aggression stems from mistreatment.

DARA WALDRON

A SHEEPDOG NAMED OSCAR

Dogs are often too eager to please, manifesting in submissive behaviour. The way Oscar bends his head when he sees me — the way he gazes up with the side of his face touching the ground — is evocative. But it is evocative, he added, because collies are so attentive to command. They look to a handler for signals. John spoke about companionship as a defining but often under-looked trait of working dogs. It was not that long ago that shepherds would spend weeks in the mountains, accompanied only by their dog. Oscar, he said, is that sort of dog. You can tell by his desire to please, movement and sensitivity to noise; his 'eye' and 'bone.' You can see the way he hunches, staring into the distance. He is bred to make things happen with his eyes.

'Look over there,' John said, pointing at the Silvermines Mountains in the distance, Keeper Hill pushing up to the sky, 'he'll be your best friend up there.' His final, near prophetic remark stuck in my mind, pushing hard against the cliché that a dog is a man's best friend. As I gazed up at the mountain that lent a shadow on John that day, the thought of hiking began to excite me again. I had lost touch with hiking over the years; I couldn't even recall my last proper hike in the hills.

John declared forcefully, 'he'll be a great companion. But it'll take time.' Maybe the Geordie intonation in his speech attracted me, or the potential passing of knowledge from one nation to another.

'How long?' I then replied in haste, trying to be exact. But the sky was starting to change colour. A greyish black cloud was masking the dulling sun. A virulent humidity encased the clouds.

'Who knows?' he responded with something of a sigh. His words were difficult to read. 'Bear in mind that Oscar had a master. Time is needed to adjust to new surroundings. Everything's new. The more invested he was before, the longer it will take for a new attachment to form. His owner may not have been nice, who knows, but he was the only one Oscar knew.' Facial lines, wrinkles even, appeared like tree rings in front, traces fostering the perception that his lived experience was in the process of passing from John's generation to mine. I turned John's words over on the drive home, as my new dog shivered in the back. The word 'companion' buzzed in my head like a fly on a summer night. Perhaps the time would come when the groomed sheepdog in the back seat would be content to run the trails with his new friend. I whispered to Oscar. But it was hard to know whether my words were of any real solace, whether repeating them over made any real difference.

We planned to walk a five-kilometre loop through Glenstal estate with Oscar that evening, tempering back along the road to the village. The route moves through beautifully manicured grounds. A manmade lake homing a family of swans sits on the right-hand side of the driveway, acres of farmland to the left and right inhabited by grazing cattle. Centuries-old trees stagger the driveway. At the top of the mile-long driveway, a little roundabout runs counter to a revivalist Norman castle, now the property of the Benedictine Order. A path leads from the former Barrington residence, the new monastery, through the remainder of the grounds. Walkers pass sections of mature exotic forestry, a seating area where playing fields can be viewed from a preeminent position. After a kilometre, one exits the back gates onto a road that passes farmlands and country homes, residential areas, and a school. It runs back to the village close to a football pitch and the pitch and putt course across from the gates of the Abbey and situated five minutes from our house.

The route is busy throughout the year and always open to the public. Walkers are required to keep their dogs on a lead; the downside being that dogs become tense. Walkers are asked to wear high viz, so the route is an outpouring of extravagant colour. As we set off it was hard to take in the surroundings. Villagers came out to savor the summer's arrival. Ylva held on to the leash, as Oscar began pulling in a perpetual forward movement. It was a struggle to contain his unbridled enthusiasm. But it was also clear to anyone with an understanding of dogs that he was never walked in a domesticated fashion; it would take years for his perpetual transformation into a pet. As is custom, the walkway was busy. Lagging to photograph the group from behind, Oscar awkwardly stood out. Friendly to those he met on the way, he was unsure of himself. He dragged Ylva from one side of the road to the next, like a rugby player making forward carries from the back of a ruck.

The group was hunched together. It was hard to say from our body language whether we were embarrassed or proud that a not-very-good-at-walking-on-a-lead sheepdog was part of our family. Progress along the driveway was slow. The lake and swans (a sight that in its absolute wonder is sometimes difficult to distinguish as real) stood out on our right. Lush pastures littered with cattle appeared on the left. At a certain point, Oscar flopped to the ground, refusing — point blank — to budge. He crouched, his paws pushed out, his body left horizontal, head rested on the road. I took the leash from Ylva to pull him on, but his body was immobile at that point. Lurching to grab, I tried — in the sternest possible manner — to move him. I shouted, 'Oscar... move!' But he didn't react. Instead, he pushed his face sideways, staring ahead. His stubbornness evoked a time in my youth when helping my father load a horse into a horsebox. A group huddled together in the yard beside the stables, another group in support. It was a particularly stubborn horse that was clearly afraid of the horsebox. Just when it seemed there was no chance the horse would budge, even when gently whipped, he did a dance and trotted into the box. I thought about trying something similar with Oscar that would gently coax him along. But then I turned around to see a cow staring at us.

The cow was peering over the fence, quietly mulching on grass. 'Don't tell me you're afraid, Oscar,' I said, looking beyond while trying to make light of the incident. 'Let's go back,' Ylva responded anxiously, as Anton muttered, 'Don't force him, Dad.' But instead of heeding their advice, the leash slipped from my hand, and I pushed the cow to back off. Oscar retreated. There was little time to gesture at the cow to take a hike before Oscar tipped his tail against the often electrified wire, compelling him to run away as fast as he could. He ran in fear for his life. We were standing on the road as evening walkers bustled past at speed. Oscar sprinted off so fast, first into an adjacent field and then on toward the gates of the estate.

'I'll run down', I said, 'Anton, you go in through the field.' Ylva stayed put on the driveway in case he returned. Panic set in. He had yet to be properly micro-chipped; had no nametag. He could take off anywhere. 'I've scared the life out of him with my stupidity. He'll be in Cappamore before we get near the gate,' I muttered, running to the gates that we passed through minutes earlier.

'Don't frighten him, Dara, he seems terrified of cattle,' Ylva shouted after me as I motored down the hill, the lake now to my left. Passing through the front gates again, I hesitantly took the road to my right leading to the Clare Glens — the famous waterfalls that act as a border between Limerick and Tipperary — passing farms and standalone cottages. I then decided to turn and run towards the village. Bellowing out Oscar's name as loud as I could, hoping he would recognise my call and forget the cattle that he had just ran from, the words, 'Dad, are you there?' echoed out from behind the eight-foot wall standing beside me. 'What?' I shouted, slowing down, still unsure of who or where the person was speaking from. A group of women decked out in sprightly coloured walking apparel began drifting towards me, chatting loudly before politely stepping aside to let me pass as I ran past them in a sweat. They could see that I was in a panicked state about something or other. But I was far too perplexed to salute back at them. It was only when the group had passed me by that I was able to call out aloud, 'Anton?' Anton then instantly replied, 'Over here, Dad.'

The wall towered over me to such a degree it shrunk my sense of self. The trees' plumage dripped over the stone. A mysterious world beckoned to me; like stepping through a wardrobe. 'Is Oscar in there?' I asked from a trance-like state. A neighbour then waved at me from his garden across the street, pointing a stick in the air. A 'thank you' tempered back in his direction when in the process of locating a gate. 'Trying to find the dog, lads,' I shouted back, as the gate appeared in front of me, beside which was a path to a tiny, forested area from where Anton was calling, Anton standing motionless on the forest path. A trail pointed in one direction, as a second meandered away in the other. About five hundred yards from our house was a forest I had no idea even existed.

'Maybe he's there somewhere, Anton?' I said, guessing, on the basis that two trails pointing in opposite directions furnished something of a loop. It was unlikely to be a large, forested area, given it backed out onto the road from where we had come. I could see it was part of the grounds that we had just walked. 'You can go that way, I'll go this way,' I said, taking my phone from my pocket to check for any recent updates. I then ran along the trail route in something of a circular fashion, left to right. I ran past a small slipstream, from where it was possible to gaze at the driveway we had come from. The trail then led to another trail, through a small thicket of thorny briars.

I ran in hope Oscar would reappear. Guilt drove me. Maybe it was my fault he ran away. Why return if sensing he was exposed to harm? I imagined him on his way, finding — in that mysterious sixth sense — a way back to his home. Then a story that was once told to me by my father, about my grandfather, about a gun dog who went missing when grandad was shooting in a bog on a summer's night — returning to the family home three weeks later in mysterious circumstances — entered my consciousness like a dream. I tried to recall the precise details of the story. It was an oracle sent to dampen anxiety. Suddenly, Anton ran past, zooming around the corner waving his hands.

'Stop, Dad,' he said, crashing into my chest. He stumbled to a standstill.

'What is it?' I replied, trying to catch my breath. 'Did you find him?' Anton pointed over at the wall, beyond which there was a footpath we just travelled on to the forest, and then further on again to our house.

'Mam said to go back home, I assume she found him.'
'She didn't say?'

I propositioned him to answer while grabbing his shirt sleeve to get his attention; surmising that Oscar was knocked over and Ylva didn't want to tell me by phone. The path garnished a new purpose, large bushes of briars and thorns announcing themselves to my flesh. A child and his mother ran quickly around the corner, saluting to us while passing. An impending disaster brought a leggy walk to a stroll, feet dragging on as I said hello in return.

We then stepped through a small inlet — full of briars — used to enter and exit the forest from the street. My mood dampened on regaining my breath to push through the opening. We walked in silence at first, glad to have found a forest five hundred yards from home but sensing bad news and the return preparation for its delivery. I didn't know whether the forest would ever be used in the way I had imagined as a place to walk a dog; I didn't know if I even had a dog to walk with. The hedges at the turn home hemmed us in, as the steely white gates of our house appeared as a haven. We turned the corner in full. Ylva was waving over at us. She had an upbeat demeanour.

'Come up here,' she declared, 'you're not going to believe where he is.'

'Where?' I said, unable to contain my enthusiasm. I was a bag of nerves.

Along our driveway, the newly planted shrubbery is

A SHEEPDOG NAMED OSCAR

harnessed by pebbles. The pebbles stapled in the driveway beside the garage and shed. In summer, swallows can be seen swooping down from leylandii trees folding in on the shed on both sides; the branches stretching to the sky. Beyond the two sheds again is a large field sitting in counterpoint to the village, beyond which the Murroe-Boher GAA pitch, Harty Park, can be seen. A church spiral edges up into the sky, a marker for those passing through the village. As Anton and I wandered up the drive, the sun pushed through the clouds to form a pink silhouette of sky, the sunset announcing itself as both magical and sublime. My feet began to pick up speed as I lifted my head to survey the parameters of the garden.

At the top of the estate, I could see the patio transformed into Oscar's bedroom apartment. Oscar was sitting outside, wagging his tail exuberantly at the door. I dropped my phone, harness, lead, and ran to him. The clasp of his coat, that of a dog assumed to have run away to never return, breached my guarded emotions. Sitting motionless in my arms, his stoical pose seemed to usher the words 'not to worry.' As arms wrapped around him in turns, his demeanour changed instantly: the comforting effect of averted disaster. Ylva had returned home as we went in search of Oscar in the forest. When she returned, in a disheveled state, he was cocked at the door to his room. Whatever happened, whatever impact the shock had had on him, he returned home. He looked up at her, with gentle eyes, suggesting he knew that something was up, before lifting his front paw in a gesture of forgiveness.

He wanted above all, at least it seemed, to be forgiven for having run off.

The reason for running off was never revealed. Something triggered him. But whatever it was it did not equate (in his eyes) with those who had taken him from the farm and set up camp for him in a new home: our family. This perhaps insignificant observation on my part brought a degree of happiness with it. Yes, I was happy the catastrophe had been averted. But I was happy, beyond everything, home was starting to mean something to Oscar. He trusted enough in me to return *home*. Of course, considerable time was taken up speculating why he had stopped suddenly in his tracks on the driveway. Was it the cow at the fence that scared him? Or the shock from the fence?

Our big takeaway from the ordeal was the 'time before' to speculate on. No matter how much we wanted to discover the truth, we would never be certain of the before. The next day, as I had planned, I raised the issue with the town vet, a quiet man who spoke slowly but always on point. It was our first meeting, and to travel to his clinic I had to carry Oscar into the car. I opened the back door of the car in the vet car park in the middle of Newport village. A small ball of poo fell out of the car in sync with Oscar leaping from the back seat. The poor guy shat himself. And he was shivering. I cleaned the mess up and spent the next few minutes coaxing him into the vet's waiting room. When we finally got in to see the vet, too frazzled to remember about the stuff the previous evening, the vet did a body check, registering, microchipping, and vaccinating Oscar, then feeling for lumps; everything to make him a pet. He opened a file on the clinic computer and discussed the term 'working dog' for his 'breed' section. The words sheepdog and worker stuck in my mind.

More jigsaw pieces fell into place. Oscar is a dog bred to work livestock. Not just sheep, but cattle. Blind dogs, sled dogs, hunting, and mountain rescue. Dogs that guard stuff. Sniffer dogs. Medical assistance dogs. Therapy dogs. Herding dogs. Workers. The vet had specified the breed as collie, but the talk of worker and 'sheepdog' for his file seemed to suggest border collie. More research into the world of dogs was required. The more I read up on the matter, the more research I did on working dogs, the more expansive the description of the category became. All kinds of sheepdogs herd livestock. Herding dogs are not just border collies. Kelpies, Australian Shepherds, Old English Sheepdogs herd and qualify as workers. A rabbit hole was emerging into which I temporarily fell. The shenanigans at Glenstal, when Oscar stopped in his tracks before a cow leaning over a fence, began to take on meaning. Maybe Oscar had been trained to herd livestock; is he a cattle dog that had never made the grade? Maybe he was a dog who simply didn't graduate as he was expected. Something happened; set him off and he was terrified of cattle as a result.

The sheepdog description recalled the haunting loss felt reading the Prologue to Eileen Battersby's memoir *Ordinary*

Dogs. Battersby tells of her journey through life with her rescue dogs. The Prologue recalls a holiday on a favoured Connemara beach, when a recently deceased sheepdog is discovered by her dogs behind a dune. The carcass of the animal drained of life haunts the text, a life other to that of Battersby's own canine companions, who do not have to work for their keep.

The life of a sheepdog, like the ghost filtered from Battersby's book, began to obsess me. Why had Oscar quivered in fear? Why had he run away? What was it? I googled 'working dogs,' 'cattle dogs' when sat in my car, as all sorts of hits about collies and shepherds, Kelpies and McNabs returned. But I needed to move. The sun was pushing in through the clouds and the temperatures were becoming uncomfortable. It was not even midday, and the thermometer was already reading twenty-four degrees Celsius. I reversed slowly out of the car park and headed for home. Hitting off in the direction of the Centra Station on the outskirts of Newport, I approached the turn to Murroe. Just then cattle appeared, in an echo of the previous evening's outing. It was strange to think that my dog was afraid of cattle. Was Oscar kicked when training to herd? If so, had he undertaken considerable training? Back at the house, I turned to peer in the backseat at a dog who was slowly encompassing a much desired responsibility. I had a real desire to learn about his past: his farm life. 'Oscar,' I said, as he wagged his tail, like something buffering to jump from the car as fast as he could, 'did you get kicked in the head from a cow? What happened to you in Clare?'

Pretty soon the past was a mystery I had to solve, an obsession to fix. The mystery needled more and more. Going by the vet's inspection that day, Oscar was around four years old at the time. That meant four years unknown to me; four years that were a big blurry mystery. The silent protest at Glenstal was a pointer to his pre-life existence, the past pushing through in behavioral characteristics. It was an invitation to speculate about where he came from. He had recoiled in fear at the sight of cattle. He had then made it abundantly clear he was going nowhere near them. He didn't growl, become aggressive; nor did he whimper and cry. Instead, he displayed a remarkable ability to recoil into a lump of mass. His ability to unpack the weight of his body of vital forces, to 'play dead' as the posture is known in collie lexicon, was fascinating in itself: a web of research I was soon entangled in around a world of herding dogs. A sheepdog was waiting at his patio 'office' when I was running frantically to find him through a forest, one I didn't know existed.

The forest: *another* discovery of our evening walk.

Spatial orientation is a type of intelligence that never fails to elicit amazement. It is led by scent. We hadn't even brought Oscar to the field at the back of our garden, a pathway through the trees, yet he found his way back in record time. Like a homing pigeon sensing its way, he has an innate ability to orient to an origin. He ran, perhaps shocked by the

DARA WALDRON

fence, through a looped walk of the unknown forest onto a road connecting the estate to another leading from Murroe to Newport. The same intelligence that helped him to survive on a derelict farm for more than six weeks, after possibly being abused, helped him to orient his way back home. Some dogs like to hunt, losing themselves in the scents that guide their movements in so many different directions at once — like our Labrador family dog I had spent hours as a teenager enticing out of parklands when engrossed in the retrieval processes — but others, like Oscar, return to their master at all times: they run away into the distance in order to circle back to the exact point of origin from where the master instructs.

Oscar's file stated, 'working dog.' 'Sheepdog' was an equivalent descriptor. The vet had drawn these conclusions from working in the company of dogs. He typed in Oscar as a longhaired black and white collie with (dominant and) traditional black and white markings. These markings are generally thought to be the classic marking of a border collie. Symmetrical white lines divide his face with a full white-collar spread around his neck. Four white 'socks' accompany a white sleeve on his right leg. Border collies are generally distinguished by their coat length and markings, black and white being the dominant colour along with a medium length coat. But the dogs come in blue and red merle, tricolour (black, brown, and white), piebald, ginger, and lilac. Such diverse colouring makes it is difficult to distinguish a Border Collie from Australian Shepherd or a Welsh Sheepdog. Hair length is also a significant identifier: long-haired collies shed their hair throughout the seasons. A double layered coat keeps them cool throughout hot summer months. Long-haired black and white sheepdog collies like Oscar tend to suffer more than most in hot climates, as the indexed terrain for a sheepdog/border collie is the wet and cold mountainous border land between England and Scotland — the border country from where border collies take their name. Short-haired border collies/sheepdogs are also commonly found across Ireland and the British Isles. They share the same DNA as their longhaired brethren, but they have a smoother and obviously shorter mane.

As such, border collies exist in all shapes and sizes. They are dogs, known simply as 'collies.' The breed's popularity in Ireland and the British Ilse comes from the successful TV show *One Man and His Dog* — one of the most watched series of my childhood, about the trialing escapades of shepherd and dog. The show feeds into *Country Life*, another dedicated to the British countryside. Like a window into rural life, *One Man and His Dog* is a monument to farming traditions and herding dogs indigenous to Britain and Ireland, a show that has enthralled the public on both sides of the Irish Sea for several decades. I began researching border collies and sheepdogs during those first months at a time when borders — negotiations for Brexit kicking off around the time Oscar entered our life — were in the news, and in reference to the refugee crisis in Europe. Syria and Greece were front page, perking more considered interest in borders as liminal 'spaces' that divide one landmass from another. Was there any other creature — canine or otherwise — I surmised, that is named after the border between two nations? An animal whose very origin is not a nation as such, but the hinterland 'between'? Is it even possible to determine the point of origin for something with a relational form? Like a place that is neither 'this' *nor* 'that'? A site neither 'here' *nor* 'there'? Was Oscar akin to a refugee, in search of an origin yet never properly feeling at home?

'Border collie/sheepdog' was the breed's name categorising Oscar as a canine 'refugee' with an estimated age of four. Neither age nor the breed is a verifiable fact about Oscar's life. These mere estimates are from a short physical inspection. Verifiable data can be attained through a DNA test but without the necessary expense to hand I began to learn about sheepdogs as best I could online. Episodes of *One Man and His Dog* uploaded on YouTube were my main resource. The TV show's pivotal attraction is trials in the symbiosis that form between animals and humans: a team (opposed to a kind of Darwinian rivalry between organisms). Filming trials in full, the show involves finding the best team. A shepherd/handler sends signals to a dog, using whistling sounds and vocals to direct the movement, the greater point of which is to enable the dog to track sheep along a designated course. Although minor tonal variations help enhance the signal as communication, exceptional sensitivity to sound helps the dog pick up on it while dutifully concentrating on the task

DARA WALDRON

'1976: How DOGS understand a SHEPHERD'S WHISTLE', *One Man and His Dog*, Animal Magic | BBC Archive. YouTube.

at hand. It is not just the dog's suitability for the task that gains points, but the handler's capacity to work with the dog to achieve this goal. The relationship between the dog and handler, the way they work in tandem, is the show's considered and main attraction. The dog crouches to 'eye' the sheep, creeps from side to side, moves in circles. For some, 'eye' is crucial, for others movement. But the combination of 'eye' and movement (known as 'bone') is the mark of a team.

My interest in *One Man and His Dog*, however, was based on more than just dogs. It was the suspense of trialing that attracted me, the 'will he or won't he' involved in cheering on a dog herding sheep. From watching these episodes, I learned about the intricate bond needed between handler and dog. I understood why the dog reacts to a command. A sense of 'right' and 'wrong' is fostered in a sheepdog, when it is appropriate to crouch or stand, a training resulting from a symbiotic pact. The pact itself, however, does not emerge overnight and does not form with just anyone. It forms with someone felt to be the dog's master. The more I thought back to when Oscar recoiled in fear on our first evening walk around Glenstal estate, the more convinced I would become that something must have gotten in the way of the trust between him and his handler. He was hurt. Trust had been broken. The bond with his handler had come apart, the consequences of which are in fact stark. Perhaps Oscar ran away from his original home to the farm I found him in because the novel bond had broken. He was a product of a trust relation that had come to an end.

This bond/relationship is the focus of *Nop's Trials*, another of the texts about collies I consulted in those early days. The book is about a sheepdog/border collie called Nop stolen from the handler by a rival trialer. Nop is an exceptional stockdog who is treated well by his handler Lewis. The book details the bond between Lewis and Nop against the travails of Nop's treatment when stolen. Nop is not merely a worker, but a soul mate. The book is celebrated around the world by farmers, agility lovers, and sheepdog/border collie handlers identifying with the forlorn, sad master, Lewis.

John thought Oscar, like Nop, would become a great companion, so he must have seen his readiness to trust. He must have foreseen a bond forming between us over time. Maybe the return from Glenstal was the bond in the early stages of formation? That Oscar recognised the house as his home was also a sign? A sign of his integration? Soon after that day Oscar made his way home from our first aborted walk, something of even greater significance occurred. Something happened between us. It was evening and the light began to lose its strength. Darkness folded upon the day as I ushered Oscar into his one-bedroom patio room. I gently combed Oscar's coat in a meticulous fashion. It had become a daily ritual to keep him tidy. It was a chore to coax him into the room, not to mind the basket in the patio corner; a bed he did not recognise. It had never occurred to me a dog who had come home with us would not see his bed as *his*, but that Oscar would walk into a room and think the bed was another's. The empty

A SHEEPDOG NAMED OSCAR

'1976: How DOGS understand a SHEPHERD'S WHISTLE', *One Man and His Dog*, Animal Magic | BBC Archive. YouTube.

basket was a sad sight. To see him sleeping on cold tiles was akin to holding a mirror up to my loss. On the fourth night after he was brought home, I tip-toed into his room to see a silhouette form on the mountain through the window, captivating my gaze. Then I peered in through the window connecting the patio room to the kitchen. Pushing one foot in front of another, I nudged the curtains slightly ajar. I wanted to make as little noise as possible. My gaze fell upon a scene: Oscar sprawled in his basket. It was a black and white mess, feet pushing forward and back, like a ball of energy in slow motion. I pulled myself back, before gazing again. Four feet began jerking one way and another, suggesting uneasy sleep. But the basket was no longer empty, no longer a pitcher in the form of Guinness settling in a cold glass. I looked in upon the scene for another moment, peering in at a sight perhaps wonderful only for me. Then the picture began to blur as I struggled to grasp details. Salty tears began to fall along my cheeks.

Events that mean very little for some can be, for others, a source of immense joy. Nothing can prepare us for a gradual turn from endless perpetual sadness — an emotion that creeps upon us over time and stays unwanted — to gradual joy. It had been many months of numb bewilderment when a detached sensation pervaded my body. Only at certain moments, listening to a song, reading a poem, or watching TV, did the force of what had happened the previous summer push through the curtains of life. The real punctured the

A SHEEPDOG NAMED OSCAR

DARA WALDRON

Hans Holbein, *The Body of the Dead Christ in the Tomb* (1520–22)
Kunstmuseum, Basel, Switzerland

shutters around my emotions. The real snuck out. Pain pushed through as the weight of reality fell in upon me. As I peeked in the window at a dog sleeping in a basket, knowing a bed was found, reality became a sudden source of grace.

Small steps must have preceded a lurch into a bed. Then the moment came upon him: a bed judged to be that of another was recognized as his own. Trying to picture this event in my mind, the point in time when the object in the room assumed its intended purpose, brought immense joy. I imagined, conjured the process in my mind, the move into the basket. The sniffing around the area, sniffing my — by then — affable scent, preceded a paw dipping in. Another followed. Soon a body made itself comfortable in the basket. The transfer, the vehicle of mood affecting me in a hive of sensation, came upon me when peering in the window at a sleeping dog. It was an echo of all the times previously spent peering into Anton's and Karl's room. Looking in to see if they were asleep: memory's delicate synapses. The covers pushed up and down discreetly, signaling the simplicity of life. I could have stared for twenty minutes at the scene. A comfortably sleeping dog began releasing jewels of memory.

Then less comfortable memories began to surface: the time tip toeing up to the coffin holding my father's body in it for the duration of his wake in Cloondarone. I began to think, peering in at him, of the Holbein masterpiece *The Body of the Dead Christ in the Tomb* (1520–22). The painting sprung to mind, like it was meant to be. I had a certain suspicion of Holbein's intentions in painting the Dead Christ, holding the view that the depicted body resembled the body of an all-too-human idol. In my estimation, something was all too real about the figure of the about-to-rise Christ. Yet, Holbein's Christ *does* indeed rise, and the shock in seeing the emaciated figure comes from an understanding that Christian faith posits the figure as both human *and* divine. This is the paradox pertaining to a Christ shockingly illuminated by Holbein for the beholder.

That same memory brought me back to the morning of my father's funeral mass, during which the eulogy was written. Thinking about the things my father was drawn to later in life; neighbours dropping by and conversations drifting in different corners, renewed my thinking about Holbein's Christ. The body in the room next to me had been battered and bruised like the figure in the painting. At the coffin, I thought of writing a eulogy to 'do justice to him,' but the word 'him' was repurposed in the form of absence; it was impossible to process the absence laid out in front. I thought again of Holbein's Christ as the Christ who *will* rise. This idea, as a kind of fantasy, stayed with me long after. Perhaps to believe that the dead will rise is a remedy for grief?

Dusk fell upon the room. I was gazing through the window at a dog gently sleeping. Oscar's body took the form of a 'broken' pose, marked by degrees of comfort. Every time a leg jerked up and down, before falling again, a fuzzy warm sensation permeated my body. It returned my thinking to the lyrics of 'Shelter from the Storm,' like a siren directed from the Gods. 'I've heard newborn babies wailin' like a morning dove, and old men with broken teeth stranded without love,' the lyrics advance, the rhetorical ringing, 'do I understand your question man, is it hopeless and forlorn?' The refrain pushes out, 'come in, she said, I'll give you shelter from the storm.' Babies, old men, shelter: words that gathered meaning as a dog slept in a basket. Then the sun disappeared behind the mountains, bats flew up across the window, swooping from the trees like dabs of paint spattered on the sky. There was no point in turning the lights on and waking Oscar up. Instead, I took out my camera to capture the contours of a sleeping form, before slipping away for the night. The room was transitioning into a dusky afterlife, the sky a full spectrum of blueness.

For six months upon first moving to Murroe, I walked in the village oblivious to the forest and trail beside it. Whether Oscar ran through it during our aborted walk around Glenstal Abbey, the search for him had led Anton and I to terrain that, over the next year, became a second home to me. Irish forests are rare in number. Most are reclaimed for agricultural farmland. Ireland lacks the mass forestry of mainland Europe. Murroe Wood is the name of our address, but if you did not know of the wood behind the eight-foot wall that is a boundary between the Abbey and the village you would struggle to know where the forest begins and ends. Five kilometres to the northeast of Murroe (on the backroad to Newport in the direction of Rear Cross and Upperchurch, and then on to Thurles town itself), is one of Ireland's most impressive forest walks home to majestic waterfalls on a two-kilometre route: the Clare Glens. The Barrington family who originally built Glenstal, the estate handed to the monks by the state after the War of Independence, planted thousands of trees during their tenure. The forests are thought to have reached as far as the Glens and surrounding territory.

The Glen is, no doubt, one of Ireland's most scenic walks. The trail ascends to a sea of old oak and spruce, descending by one of the most picturesque waterfalls. The walk is beautiful and terrifying.

Mature trees untypical of the Irish landscape flank the sides. Forests are health and safety concerns in the climate era, with storms more prevalent across the island. State councils are the bodies accredited to oversee the general preservation of the Glens, and its proximity is a big reason for our settling in Murroe. Trees have crashed during storms, yet the route is always open to visitors. On the top of the Glen, from the Tipperary side (the falls form a natural border between the counties of Tipperary and Limerick), one peers over the contours of the Silvermines Mountains. On the Limerick side, the start of the Slieve Felim Way at Glenstal Wood comes into view. Ancient forestry sits upon elevated land. The forest Oscar led me to five hundred yards from our house may even have reached as far as the Glens in the nineteenth century. Populated by deer, foxes, squirrels, owls, bats, pine martens, and birds that emit the most vocal song on the island (I learned this from nature conservationists who travelled from Dublin one Sunday morning), the wood is always in close range. We can walk in minutes from a house to a forest containing all of nature's delights.

At the front gates of the Abbey, a trail leads away into the forest. It runs in a kilometre loop. The route is an island in the man-made: the village, monastery, monastery farm, shops, garages, schools, and churches. The trail extends from the gate, like a wardrobe, into another world. Tributaries cut up through the forest. Someone has even turned a ten-metre fallen tree trunk into a seat for kids to congregate at weekends. Girl guides and scouts meet in balmy summer months when the forest is in bloom and nature is infused with the gush of summer. Another trail crosses a stream, moving up along a path to the monastery. Sometimes, deer are found wandering down from higher ground to feed in this area, munching silently in the woods. Deer stumble onto the road in morning, from the opaque wilderness to the urban streets. I find it replenishing to go to the forest in the early morning, to walk or run in whatever season. It is a prompt that life is a forest to forage in. For the great Dante, the forest is a symbol of sin. Sin feeds on the need for Light. Wandering in a forest involves a search for light; the sinner grappling in the dark to find the Light.

DARA WALDRON

Forests thus have a longstanding legacy across the arts. Writers and artists use the forest to illustrate trees as essential to the environment. Forests are literary metaphors to depict heroic struggle. The beginning of the *Inferno*, as an example, contains — for many scholars — the poem's most arresting lines. 'I found myself within a forest dark,' Dante notes, 'for the straightforward pathway had been lost.' 'Ah me! how hard a thing it is to say,' he advances to 'what was this forest savage, rough, and stern.' Dante paints an image of a sinner seeking the way to God's Light. Darkness pervades the forest, but a lack of Light is what makes the forest so threatening a place.

Dante's forest retains its threats. No obvious path out of it exists. One finds in the savage bent of a wilderness, animals that can and will attack any given moment. Many of these animals are now extinct today. Those that still reside in 21st-century Irish forests live in fear of predatory humans. Many live side-by-side with human others, rarely making their presence felt. Pine martens, successfully reintroduced to Irish wildlife, thrive in the Glenstal forest Oscar and I had begun to habitually walk each morning. I had yet to see any of these creatures up close. Red squirrels, indigenous to the Irish countryside, could appear at any moment, grappling on the trail ground for acorns. I would often notice them scuttle and scamper in lightning-fast time. It was practically impossible to see them close-up. It was soon after the walk at Glenstal that Oscar and I began to make our way to the forest in the morning. It was a soon-to-be-ritual in early stages of formation.

The ritual walk takes about an hour. On our way to the forest, a little gate appears, at the wall situated around the corner from our home. Oscar steadfastly pulls on the leash until we arrive at the gate. Once he has passed through it, he is allowed to run off leash. We then saunter in an anti-clockwise direction, trudging around a bend before angling back the other direction, the gradient lifting. Passing the bigger trees to our right — the loop nearing its conclusion — Glenstal Abbey stands out in the distance. The presence of walkers on the driveway has a soothing effect on me. It fashions a sense of camaraderie. One is part of all that appears lacking in the greater preserve of forest: the human. For our first forays in the area, Oscar stayed on his leash, jerking and dragging along. The smell of dogs lured him like a magnet. He was taken in by scent.

Those first few days I kept him on a leash to stop him from running off. Dog walking has altered so much since walking dogs as teenagers in a local park. Letting dogs run free, especially medium sized like Oscar, is increasingly difficult in Irish townships. The time when dogs were allowed to wander freely, unbeknownst to their owners, with the kind of independence that often saw them take off for days to then return hungry, is a distant memory. Laws have passed to inhibit wandering in townships and farmers are much more adept at controlling unattended animals in the countryside with poison. My teenage dog walking days were spent coaxing a Labrador from a river, her instinct to swim a bane of my life. Hours were also spent trying to find the smaller dog. Whole afternoons were spent searching in yellow gorse for a bitch Jack Russell, unfussed by her size in comparison to others.

For those first excursions, Oscar jerked his head back and forth. Gaining enough confidence, he was then given enough license to run free. That he stayed within a distance, looked for a command, meant it was not long before overconfidence set in. Oscar ran off around a bend, only to, at a point when I would lose sight, hunch, and wait, typical of a sheepdog. On our fourth morning in the forest, consumed by work and accustomed to a pattern of running off and waiting, I reached a bend. Oscar was gone. I called his name. He did not return. Suddenly I was bellowing his name in the middle of a forest on the edge of the village. Screams and whistles followed, neither of which did anything. I began to run the forest loop at speed. I did a loop, but to no avail. Next, I ran up the middle of the oak-laden area, before taking off down a patch of the woods where teenagers congregate on summer evenings; but he still wasn't there. Then, thinking of our earlier debacle at Glenstal, I sprinted off in the direction of home, all the while trying to maintain a level of calm.

Neighbours were standing together on the street across the street. 'Did you see a black and white sheepdog?' I shouted in their direction. A communal 'no' was returned. In panic, still hollering his name, I thought of driving in the car in search of him when, for some reason, and on the spot, I returned to the woods through the field adjacent to a pub just behind our house. The briars cut my skin as I kneeled over a hedge that left scrape marks on my hands, before tiptoeing through the soon-to-be-cut grass in front of a thicket of green reconfigured as a boundary. A bar had been repurposed as a gate of entrance for the football and hurling pitch. The bar needed to be pushed over to the side and the briars kicked in before I was on the muddied path that leads to an old derelict concrete car park. Oscar still did not appear. I thought again about running back to the gate at the forest opening from where I had just come (from the opposing direction), when my neighbour Davey appeared out in front of my sightline. He was standing on the road. He was waving his arms in my direction. As my legs pushed on towards where he stood, his stick pointed at the small gate I had walked through. It was like a scene from a genre action movie. I was the manic detective chasing a criminal to a forest at the edge of town. I was laughing and crying.

    I ran up the middle of the road, not even sure why I was running in that specific direction. Leaping onto footpath I advanced through the gate, shouting 'thank you' in Davey's direction. Inside, like the meaning had arrived before a poem's end, Oscar appeared. He ran over to me, tail wagging at an electric rate. He jumped up, deflating the tension

A SHEEPDOG NAMED OSCAR

DARA WALDRON

immediately. I tagged a leash on him before turning to Davey who was standing before me. My breathing slowed down in degrees. I stopped.

'I saw him nudge the gate door,' Davey said, as his wife Bridey waved, smiling from across the road.

'I lost sight of him in the woods,' I said, more breathless than assumed, before introducing Oscar to Davey.

It was a minor crisis. Yet a friendship with my neighbours began that day. Years later, now, in the morning, Davey, Blackie and Prince, a nonagenarian neighbour and his dogs, meet us at the forest. We talk about all sorts: sport, weather, politics. And the dogs play like they have been friends since they were pups.

When human beings found out about death
They sent the dog to Chukwu with a message:
They wanted to be let back to the house of life.

—Seamus Heaney
A Dog Was Crying Tonight in Wicklow

TWO ⁑ INTO THE WIND

Mishaps continued to occur in the months after that escapade. They mainly came about when Oscar made his way to the forest. Davey would ring to say that he had seen him on route. But the roaming soon stopped. Time passed, the boundaries strengthened and the walk in the woods became a daily ritual. Oscar would run out in front before circling back. Each time he circles back he looks to me for affirmation. The outrun and return is a mantra, a rhythm that invokes — perhaps deep in the unconscious — a belief that the things that go away will eventually return. Like Nemo's eventual return home, Oscar will return to me in due course. His instinct is to return to his handler. Taken as a bond of a symbiotic nature, some unseen connection between human and nonhuman, this instinct again ignited significant curiosity in me. I set out to gather more information about the creature I was putting my faith in. Collies, as a common breed across Ireland, have DNA that can be traced to some of the earliest incarnations of agricultural life on the island itself; back to a time when sheep and cattle farming was first practiced in the green pastures of the Emerald Isle.

'Collie', according to some genealogies of the word, derives from the ancient Gaelic 'coileán.' The theory goes that collies originated in Ireland with monks who later fled to Scotland. In modern dictionaries, collie is cited in plural as 'colaí' while in others it is the singular 'sípéar.' The ancient meaning of coileán is 'pup,' believed to encapsulate the idea of a dog that helps. A coileán is a helper, a pup who is by your side. Perhaps the bond between coileán, (or even in the modern vernacular sípéar as *sheepdog*), and handler was consolidated in centuries past when sheepdogs would spend weeks in the mountains with handlers. Collies are not single beings in this sense, but shadows: symbiotic, plural entities. Collie, in addition, is the English vernacular description for a canine type. Friends ask, Is Oscar a collie?' and I hesitate to reply 'yes.' I have no definitive proof. There is no paper stating Oscar is this or that. Going by the vet's analysis, Oscar is best defined as a working sheepdog collie. My research into the heritage of sheepdogs across Ireland and Britain had given me a general understanding of the kind of dog associated with the word 'collie.' It had given me a relatively good understanding of Oscar's behaviour. The constant looping in the forest began to make sense. The wait at the front door at eight o'clock every morning, pent up with excitement to get going to the forest, began to make sense. The crouch and stare, when making his way towards other dogs, began to make sense. His unwavering concentration on an object, moving through wide-open expanses at the back of our house, began to make sense. The eyes staring up at me when a bowl is put in his patio room, waiting for me to leave before eating, also made sense.

Though so much made sense regarding the collie/coileán, something about my relationship with Oscar went beyond the specificities or category 'breed.' Something got in the way of the associated criteria. Breeds, after all, are defined by traits, but they can fail to get at the greater entanglements around human beings and dogs. If it is true that a big proportion of people anthropomorphize dogs as pets, it is also probably true that certain breeds are more inclined to enter companion relationships with human beings. And one of these breeds is undoubtedly the collie. Maybe, I surmised, to fully understand Oscar's personality, as I would come to confidently call it, I needed to understand the kind of pact, the symbiotic states, that collies enter into with other beings.

A set of events once told to me by a friend, when we were both carefree university students, came back to me at this time. My friend returned to Connemara every summer to work at a co-operative of farmers and fishermen outside Roundstone. In those months, one of the farmers would ramble into the shop accompanied by a sheepdog. The bond was striking. Rope was cast as a ready-made leash to keep the dog in check. The coileán would sit at the door waiting as the farmer passed through the shop for weekly provisions.

DARA WALDRON

A SHEEPDOG NAMED OSCAR

One Friday, the story went, workers congregated in the pub where it was traditional to mark the end of week. When a farmer arrived and started drinking excessively at the bar, one of the workers inquired if someone in the village had died. Somebody answered that the farmer's sheepdog had passed. I thought back to this story, set in a time and place that had enchanted my younger self and had stuck with me. The setting was heavily removed from the life I inhabited at the time. My friend had become fascinated by the unspoken grief that coalesced around the farmer and his dog's sudden absence. My mind became an anchor, fishing in rivers of time, unearthing analogies to help explain the trust evolving between a sheepdog and me.

Oscar waits for me to return from work. He waits at the gate, his sense of time unperturbed by waiting. I arrive home to a black and white form crouched on his stomach: a ritual of sorts. Oscar waits attentively for the car to appear at the gate. As these rituals mounted, a dog waiting on my return, and morning walks in the woods grew rapidly in length and frequency, I began to dwell upon the story told to me so many eons ago. I pictured the farmer my friend described entering a small rural pub, his head bowed beneath a woolen cap, his wellingtons covering ragged trousers. I imagined the farmer edging over to the bar to order his first drink. No words are spoken, and a finger is used to order a pint. A drink is served, and then the farmer presses his fingers against the chilled glass. No words come from his chapped lips. He sits cradling his drink and then he orders another. An hour passes in the pub while he drinks heavily on his own. The pub begins to fill up, and the farmer begins to work the room in a drunken state, talking to punters who have congregated for the evening. He cuts a sullen figure alone, pacing around the pub with no one to think of but his lonesome self.

The scene stirs my imagination. At no time is the farmer heard mention his dog Jess. Diagnosed with cancer, within weeks the dog passed away. Some farmers know; nobody dares to console him. I imagine the farmer in an increasingly drunken state, lifting a whiskey glass in the air in salutation. 'To Jess,' he splutters to himself, stumbling out the door inebriated. The farmers talk about mourning a dog named Jess who travelled with the farmer everywhere. I imagine my friend beside his father, taking in an experience that passes to me as anecdote. It is a story that, for some reason, stays with me. What are the terms of the farmer's grief? Is love the real ruse of his pain?

It is closing time when he stumbles along a country road that straddles the Connemara village of Roundstone, venturing back into his own sea of absence. He passes a choppy Galway Bay, the crashing water a hammer to his gut, a mantra for his newfound loneliness. He walks along the seashore, stumbling one way and then another, seagulls circling overhead against an elevated moon. Silence is pressing, taking form as nature's music: waves crashing and the wind circulating in the surrounding aether. The farmer kicks seaweed

A SHEEPDOG NAMED OSCAR

Photo: Joachim Kohler.

to the side of the road, shouts the word 'Jess' into the wind. And then he stops to sit awhile on the rocks leading down to the seashore.

He is silent. A small boreen is lit up in the moonlight. His body shuffles across the boreen, as moments of clarity interrupt sustained falling movements. Soon he arrives at a white cottage with a newly painted door, behind which is a large, corrugated shed and a gate where animals can pass through. An old tractor stands idly in the moonlight. He pushes through the door and then on through another, towards a cold bed lying against brick walls. There he sleeps alone. He wakes the following morning unsure what has brought such melancholy, all-too-pervasive feeling of dread.

These events unfold as imagery of the Connemara coastline, where mountains scale to the sea and lakes sparkle in the summer sun. In winter monumental storms grip the land and hold it in their belly, as the Atlantic rain swirls over the bay, glazing the land with newly patterned puddles of rainwater. The farmer in my imagination gets up and walks out to his land, his beloved Jess no longer by his side. The fields are not the same; life has changed in an instant. All too vibrant in its speculative form, the anecdote burst to life as a kind of dream. It came to me in pictures that centered on the interdependence of life. The story of a sheepdog brought me to a world where care transmits in more than one direction; a world where animals and humans coexist in symbiotic states; yet a world where most animals are readied for the slaughter.

A SHEEPDOG NAMED OSCAR

Sheepdogs are called upon throughout the day. Work is a pact between the nonhuman and human. Dogs take form as symbiotic companions, moving animals that live in counterpoint to them. But what if the world of farm animals and pets are not so separate? What if farm animals live as domesticated extensions of a companion's self? The human and animal world — this is what struck me when sketching out the life of a lonely bachelor farmer in the corridors of Connemara — is not so naturally opposed. Nature exists in the form of symbiosis. The care a dog returns to a handler played over and over when contemplating 'Jess.' My farmer is sad and lonely grieving the passing of who, or what? A friend? A real person? He is hungover and numb as he digs a hole in the earth. The rain brushes his eyes, the wind blows his cap this way and that. Clay sticks to an iron shovel. The hole he digs is two feet. When he finishes digging, I imagine the farmer drawing a refuse sack from a wheelbarrow that holds the body of Jess, before lowering the carcass into the grave. Rain gushes upon his face, swirling in a gale; daggers directed from the Atlantic. There are no tears.

The famer mutters obscenities about paying a vet to dispense an animal carcass no one wants, content that she rests in the backfield beneath a tree parallel to larger fields. The hole is mechanically overladen with muck and clay until barely noticeable. Words mumble from lips shuddering with cold, 'You were special, go off and run the fields.' There is nothing more to say. My farmer takes out a few splintered pieces of wood, tied together in the middle with a piece of rope. He places the cross object at the center of a little mound, perking up from the ground. The grave is barely noticeable on grass overladen with scratchy patches of green. Then the farmer kneels in the mud, his wellingtons sticking in the ground as the rain belts in upon him. Muffled talk — 'in heaven' ... 'kingdom come' ... 'daily bread' — bring forth words that soon evaporate into a wind that bites into his beleaguered soul.

And then, at this moment the farmer stands up. He walks over to a gate above which grey clouds push over the bay and a radiant sun veers out from beneath. He buries his hands in his pockets. He climbs the steps beside a gate to return home. It is his first day alone in fifteen years. Cake and tea are waiting for him at home. It will be months before he mentions her name; before he drives to Clifden to view a sheepdog pup.

Canine companions play a role in literature across the ages, from the classic literary texts like *Lassie* to the more recent *Drive Your Plough Over the Bones of the Dead* by Polish Nobel Laureate, Olga Tokarczuk. Animal rights is a tributary running through Tokarczuk's murder mystery, impacting purposefully upon the narrative. The novel is a detective story set at the border between Poland and the Czech Republic, the protagonist a spinster by the name of Janina Duszejko. Janina's dogs go missing from her home before Big Foot, her neighbour, and a well-known hunter, is found dead by her friend Oddball. The protagonist suspects murder. Janina writes to the authorities to suggest the animals committed 'murder' as revenge for the hunters deeming them to be subservient beings. As the plot thickens, a priest, Father Rustle, who Janina challenged in his support of hunting, is found dead. Suspicion intensifies, implicating Janina as a suspect. At this point the text takes a significant turn to the left, as her missing murdered dogs become the novel's central focus.

Drive Your Plough Over the Bones of the Dead is a strange hymn to the nonhuman. Tokarczuk deconstructs the moral hierarchies of 'nature' that relegate the nonhuman to the shadows of the natural realm. It is like the world is altered so that Janina's nonhierarchical way of seeing is included. A photograph revealing the murdered priest standing over his hunted prey, including Janina's two dead dogs, takes the form of the textual McGuffin. In the novel's conclusion, Janina admits to the murder of revenge. The story ends with the anti-heroine fleeing Poland for the Czech Republic, having confessed her crime.

The nonhuman 'other' as person is the central focus, the novel positioning the reader to apportion a boundary between nonhuman and human. 'Why is the killing of a deer mere sport, and the killing of a human murder?' Sarah Perry's *Guardian* review of the novel asks, 'and if animal rights are elevated to those of human rights, would animals then be subject to criminal and human law — if an animal can be said to have been murdered, might it equally be charged with murder? What, moreover, are we for?' Perry challenges us to think of nonhuman murder. The novel's world puts this moral concern at the core of life. It is a tale that directs the reader to the borderline between nonhuman and human life: the intimate border itself.

Tokarczuk's tale returned my thoughts to the Connemara farmer burying his beloved collie. I sketched it all to question whether it is possible to love the nonhuman. Love of this kind, certainly, appears to drive Janina's passion. Hunting is a cowardly aberration. As a boy I was integrated into a West of Ireland fox hunting tradition (since subsequently banned on animal welfare grounds in the UK), hunting regularly with my father on horseback. My grandfather passed on a love of the countryside to my father who encouraged hunting in his children. Like my grandfather, my father cherished being in the countryside. From age ten to fourteen I was a member of the North Galway Hunt, participating on several occasions. My love of dogs made the cruelty involved in hunting unpalatable. In my teenage years, I rebelled against the aberration of a 'sport' I later came to revise my opinion of. As a young adult I began to think of hunting as placating humanity's animal urges. Hunting, I surmised, is an outlet for fundamental human aggression. To repress, the feisty philosopher in me argued, in the guise of abstracted morality, is to sever the human from its primal origins.

I sourced animal rights studies to put my reasons to the test: Jonathan Safran-Foer's journey into the meat industry in *Eating Animals*, Peter Singer's bible for animal rights activists, *Animal Liberation*. Several of the Welsh philosopher Mark Rowlands's books were more than intriguing points of discussion, in particular his philosophical memoir about an eleven-year relationship with a pet wolf called Brenin. I thought hard about the moral sentiments put forward in these books. The animal husbandry Safran-Foer shines a light on is challenging in its descriptive horror, bringing the reader close to the unworldly conditions of the meat-eating industry. I wept at the bond that severs between Rowlands and his companion wolf Brenin when the latter dies, the text born of a love so eloquently described in the final months of Brenin's life. It is probable these passages, when an ever more reclusive Rowlands and his interspecies pack (Brenin, Nina and Tess) move to the South of France, helped develop my own interest in love in interspecies relationships. As something of an eccentric misanthrope, I too identified with the journey Rowlands describes; the *philia* apportioning to the relationship between human and wolf. As Rowlands suggests, '*philia* — the love appropriate to your pack — is the will to do something for those who are of your pack even though you desperately won't want to do it, even though it horrifies and sickens you, and even though you may have to pay a very high price for it, perhaps heavier than you can bear.'

The Philosopher and the Wolf bore heavily upon me as an influence. So too did my teenage days in pursuit of a fox, another form of *philia*: the collective energy of the hunt. The adrenaline rush on horseback — the intensity of the hunt.

DARA WALDRON

Hunting, I surmised as a university ethics student, unburdens repressed urges. Hunting, abhorrent to many, confronts the wild in all, the tether line between human and animal. I found sentiments echoed in the strangest of places, a book on hunting by English philosopher Roger Scruton. Scruton is a conservative thinker I had a particular distaste for. However, his book on hunting, read when teasing out my thinking, chimed with a memory of adrenaline rushes advancing in the countryside of East Clare on my pony Shadow. There was something intrinsically liberating about the collective pursuit of humans and nonhuman animals blending into the collective imbroglio of the pack. For Scruton, this was life-enhancing, and the experience forced him to reconsider his whole approach to nature as a result. 'The blood of another species flows through your veins,' he writes of the collective hunt on horseback, 'stirring the old deposits of collective life, releasing pockets of energy that a million generations laboriously harvested from the crop of human suffering.' At thirteen I lacked the vocabulary to describe the feelings that Scruton designates here, the hunt as immersion in the now of human and animal existence that somehow, against the protestations, seemed right. I would later recalibrate this view.

It was one of the more difficult animal rights-based studies, *Zoopolis* by Sue Donaldson and Will Kymlicka, that forced my hand. In the book, a model and theory of nonhuman citizenship is theoretically proposed. Animals, from the domestic to wild, are explored around the idea of 'flourishing' as the *form* of a sentient life. To what extent does an animal flourish according to a way of being is the abiding concern. This concern, in a nutshell, is a moral quandary. As I made my way through the dense passages, 'flourishing' began to needle as a concept. A desire for Oscar to flourish in the way described by the authors was enticing as a mode of personhood. *Zoopolis* might not be a book to everyone's tastes, but it does reveal a nonhierarchical relationship between humans and nonhumans that was most applicable to the nonhierarchic relationship I initiated between Oscar and me. I was particularly uncomfortable with the kind of bow-down authority a lot of the sites dedicated to keeping pets seemed to advocate as a best practice. I wanted Oscar to come to me because he wanted to come to me, not because I was feeding him with canine treats.

Keeping pets as prisoners bothered me when growing up as a teenager whose father had a horse farm in urban Ireland. Farmers and the travelling community were the ones I watched build relationships around activities with domestic animals on farms and hunts. Fox hunters invested time on the land in differing capacities as forms of nurture, unlike protesters I saw criticizing their sport from urban settings. Many farmers considered themselves part of a greater ecosystem. And yet, my moral concerns brewed when fox blood was painted on my face. These concerns, to one degree or other, bubbled over with Oscar. Every morning, he waits for me, his body a clock that pulsates on the chime of 8:15 a.m., helping reevaluate the essence of animal-human relations. Maybe the truth is the 'relations' — the border point where one organism dissolves into another.

In this regard, American feminist philosopher Donna J. Haraway, and British nature writer and author of bestselling *H is For Hawk*, Helen MacDonald, offer furtive explorations of the relationality between human and nonhuman. Haraway explores the synergy between dogs and humans in *The Companion Species Manifesto*. 'Telling a story of co-habitation, co-evolution, and embodied cross-species sociality,' she notes, 'the present manifesto asks which of two cobbled together figures — cyborgs and companion species — might more fruitfully inform livable politics and ontologies in current life worlds.' Haraway's key point of emphasis is 'companionship' as a canine-human criterion that compels our recording of stories of care. MacDonald, on the other hand, is drawn to the wild, the near untamable bird of prey, the goshawk. When faced with the sudden loss of her father, MacDonald is drawn to the absolute 'otherness' of this bird. The training endeavour, a rollercoaster of emotion knitted into the behaviors of a wild creature, reads like a thriller. MacDonald's descent into the subculture of hawkery, with all its attendant obsessions, her desire for a kernel of recognition, is an attempt to maintain a living connection with the deceased.

An animal rescue industry has taken root in rural Ireland around the attentive problem of unwanted sheepdogs, some of whom never make it as workers. Others are the excess of dramatic change in rural practices. High energy and neurotic personalities are a difficult sell to urban households. In addition, there is little access to agility sports to stay active as advocated by Haraway. An early working title for the present project was 'S for Sheepdog,' in homage to MacDonald's excursions and attempt to process loss. MacDonald's fascination with the goshawk, expressed in expansive descriptive prose about the wild, lies, in part, in the beauty of the hunt itself. Sheepdog aesthetics, in contrast, are defined by the bending back of a prey drive in symbiosis: transforming the kill — via the intervention of humankind — into care. There is an equally alluring beauty to the entanglement of nature and culture as nature-culture, to draw on one of Haraway's many concepts.

A black and white body runs into light, a silhouette disappears into foliage melting from green to brown. It is mucky and wet even in summer. Oscar appears, from nowhere, tongue out, ears propped in anticipation of command. We are two in the form of one. As summer turns to spring and morning walks turn to excursions at sunrise, more things turned. Oscar fell in love with the car, lying in it for hours on end. Stuff rarely noticed about him began to strike me as unique: a refusal to eat until everyone was in bed, a glassy-eyed stare in my direction when leaving his bowl. He emphasised his exuberance when a leash was pulled from my pocket in morning, dancing along the driveway to the road, sometimes standing on his hind legs or running in circles. That he was so enthused by the prospect of visiting the woods, I began to film and post the videos — his pre-walk ritual, wiggling dance — to an online border collie/sheepdog forum I joined on Facebook. Over time, as our bond grew, my posts began to gather a wider audience, from Melbourne in Western Australia to Oregon in the U.S., to Carmarthen in Wales.

As I had initially posted videos to gather feedback, to learn about the specific collie breed of Oscar, I was taken aback when members wrote to say that Oscar reminded them of their beloved border collie who passed years before. One woman inquired about coming to visit Oscar when she was in Europe — to hold such a friendly and serene dog, she commented, was akin to swimming with dolphins. She wrote about her long-lost dog, Mia. Mia shepherded her through her husband's lengthy battle with cancer. Mia would wait at the door every time my friend returned from the hospice, her eyes looking up to say, 'I know.' Another forum member, an elderly retiree living in California, wrote about a collie that appeared on the side of a road one evening when he was patrolling the highways. Like the imagined farmer mourning his beloved Jess, the man spoke of his beloved Yogi. His collie was a long-lost child, a spirit who had descended upon him in his greatest hour of need. The border collie/sheepdog forum consisted of all types: urban dwellers who had taken on the challenge of keeping a city collie, juggling work with the required windows of time needed to exercise their dog;

A SHEEPDOG NAMED OSCAR

mountain rescuers who had taken a work partner home as a retiree; buck ranchers who liked to watch their sheepdog run free in the open spaces of the prairie. Farmers who had sourced a border collie puppy to work on a farm herding often saw the same dog become, over time, a deep companion of the heart. There were so many uplifting stories on the forum, so many helpful insights into a breed. That rush of excitement in Oscar when a walk beckoned is pretty much, I surmised, the rush that exhilarates a working dog when put to work.

Border collie sheepdogs are widely known for forming robust bonds with handlers. It is not unusual to find a dog and its handler in a park, the dog fixated — to a point of obsession — on a frisbee. Other canine breeds look to distract and play but collies have little interest in play once their mind is set on an object, and therefore a job. So many collies are returned to dog pounds for rehoming because an owner — who has not done their research — is put off by the dog following them around the house, staring up at them. This is normal behaviour but stuff that unsettles. People are put off by the 'eye' continuously staring in their direction, waiting on the command 'signal.'

All this means that collies need constant stimulation. Some chase all day, bereft of an off switch; suffering 'border collie collapse', they fall into a physical stupor. But mental as much as physical stimulation is vital. Perhaps Oscar's wiggling expresses joy — a morning shuffle — doing what he is bred for: to be with me in the depths of nature. His desire to be with me, instinct to run the outreach in a pear-shaped route, before returning safely, is a trait rarely encountered with dogs in my teens. I spent whole afternoons wading through the marshes of Tuam's palace grounds. Hours were spent in search of a Labrador taken in the direction of game, trying to retrieve prey in the wild. Countless more were consumed crawling through bushes, ivy-adorned walls, in search of a terrier who barked incessantly when immersed in an activity apportioning a hunt. It was nice that these dogs were led by instinct to seek and hunt. But there was something about Oscar's instinct to return to me, something about his coming into my life when he did that I could not explain. And perhaps, on some deeper spiritual level, he came into my life for a reason. I wanted to know why.

I stumbled upon the work of philosopher-poet Denise Riley around this time. When Riley's son, Jacob, unexpectedly died of a heart attack in Spain, his death brought upon her a shattering grief. After years trying to process loss, Riley wrote an essay and poetry book about her son. The book, titled *Say Something Back*, is adjoined with an essay, 'Time Lived Without Its Flow.' In both texts, grief is explored as an altered experience of time. 'Hard to put into words, yet absolutely lucid as you inhabit it daily,' Riley writes, 'this sensation of having been lifted clean out of habitual time only becomes a trial if you attempt to make it intelligible to those who haven't experienced it.'

A persistent symptom, Riley notes, is difficulty projecting

into the future. In testimony, she feels stranded in time. Her thoughts are overladen with memory. The mechanics of flow break down. Riley finds it is near impossible to describe this loss to others. 'Feelings' of atemporality are difficult to describe, a problem the poet suggests is a kind of reckoning with the limitations of language. 'I want to try, however much against the odds,' Riley notes, 'to convey only the one striking aspect: this curious sense of being pulled right outside of time, as if beached in a clear light.' I found this sentence a solace. That first year after Dad passed, I felt the same beached sensation. Life was a struggle, lifting myself to do things. 'I need a crowd of people,' Neil Young sings on his sadly beautiful 'On the Beach,' 'but I can't face them day to day.' Young's lyric is a striking invocation of the paradoxical in grief: it does not make sense. Summer edged to autumn, green morphed into golden-brown mulch. Sixteen months passed. Grief advanced from the kind of shock Riley writes of, to the heaviness of loss, a weightiness of the senses. As the seasons changed and walking in the forest with Oscar became a ritual, everything in the phenomenological world seemed to drag me to the past, to a time already lived through. I seemed to exist with both feet stuck in the past. The future was an extravagant luxury I had no way of mapping desire onto.

My experience of loss unleashed a kind of paradoxical fantasy. A higher power was pulling the strings from another world; my father brought Oscar to me. He wanted to cushion his absence. The rhetorical question, 'where have you gone?'

brought answers I retrospectively, and perhaps with the help of Riley's texts, looked upon as a kind of denial. My father, as the Irish adage goes, looked down from above. Falling upon this fantasy helped maintain belief that death itself is not an end. In fact, the person whose number is still on my phone, whose wallet is still in my locker, whose 'things' are still scattered in my garage, merely went away. Grief was made manifest in knowing someone close had died while acting like they were there, alive. In the forest, or walking and running trails, I began to fantasise that Dad was 'pulling the strings' on my life as a way of retracting the bludgeoning feelings of loss. The utter dread of loss hovered in the background, pushing through the waking thought 'he's gone', while not able to accept the 'gone for good' bit.

Maybe I accepted but could not process the forever bit. To know but not feel the repercussions of loss is the condition Riley elaborates on ('knowing and not knowing that he's dead. Or I "know" it, but privately I can't feel it to be so') in perspicuous detail. Slow to call it 'denial,' it is perhaps best filed in that category. Riley knows, has evidence to prove Jacob's death, but expects his return. What goes away *must* come back. She struggles to compute the meaning of the word 'gone.' She looks for support, tries to write, grapples with the idea of being there for a son who is suddenly not there. The same acceptance and disbelief informed my fantasy. Oscar would help. He came to me for a reason. That is, my loss was not mine.

Our morning walks soon turned to runs, an activity that all but stopped in middle age. I soon began to cherish running with a dog by my side (especially one that takes off into the distance before circling back to me). Running condensed the time needed to keep a collie active. Mountain trails became the main sources of activity. The old pilgrimage route at the Slieve Felim Way was a retreat from the daily grist. One of the country's oldest pilgrimages, the Way is more than a breathtaking route through mountains. It is a spiritual undertaking in rough terrain. Our ancestors once walked into ancient Light. The pilgrimage starts at least from the point where we began running — on the fringes of Murroe village. From there a small ascent moves to the west, pushing along hilly terrain towards the village of Toor. From this point onwards, the trail circles back towards Keeper Hill, on to the Silvermines, a village rarely mentioned in the lexicon of Irish country life but one that is perhaps closest in its genesis and form to a typical Welsh mining village.

The route passes through an eerie landscape. For the first few miles, forested sections recede into outbursts of scree, marking the upper echelons. One can gaze out over the countryside from an elevated position. The pilgrimage, forty-three kilometres in length, takes upwards of ten hours to complete on foot. I began walking sections of the route before running it with Oscar. Longer distances were soon manageable, then comfortably running for an hour. Some days we began at the car park in the woods and ran to a plateau about three kilometres on. At the scree a further two kilometres on from that, we would turn for home. At a certain landmark, one can peer over the valleys at the farmed Tipperary grasslands below. A God's eye view of bungalows, dotted white specks on a carpet of green, can be proffered from the mountain range. The return is all downhill. Running side-by-side on the return route back to the car we would gel together, the profile of animal and human reaching a rhythmic correlation. All the pent-up adrenaline pushing through me from one day to the next relented into the wind. As we ran the route home, I took the opportunity to shout out into the vacuum of the mountain range, as a lone cuckoo punctuates the silence.

One Saturday, hiking the sign-posted *Discover Ireland* route along the Slieve Felim, the road forked in two directions. A purple sign pointed to the circuit from the car park starting point. Another of the signs indicated a pathway drifting down the mountain to some unknown destination. The completely barren land was marked by a rugged topography. Culled trees gave the appearance of a post-apocalyptic landscape taken from a sci-fi B movie. Oscar ran ahead along an incline, moving past tree stubs rotting in a man-altered landscape. Then he took off in another direction, sprinting with all the speed he could muster. He shifted gears rapaciously. A light seemed to turn on in his brain. He ran at an incredible speed. It was like a spell had been cast upon him. His silhouetted shape disappeared on the horizon, dissolving into a fog laden land. For some reason, in that moment, the degree to

DARA WALDRON

A SHEEPDOG NAMED OSCAR

which I had come to lean on him revealed itself in full.

I looked at Ylva.

'What will I do? Just stay here?' Instead, I left her and went on, dropping the bag and stick to sprint along the boreen adjacent to the field Oscar had just run through. A spate of recently culled trees led down towards a seemingly distant abyss before which my body relented to an anxious standstill. My dog, wherever he had gone, seemed to have vanished into thin air.

Panic had rooted itself and began to rise, like a train pushing slowly up a hill. Then, on one of the oldest pilgrimages, a story my father once told me as a child about my grandad shooting in a bog on the border between Galway and Mayo rushed to consciousness, full of minute detail. Darkness was falling. Grandad was deep in concentration, his German Pointer sitting by his side. On the horizon was a light. Unsure where the car was, he made his way towards the light. But it seemed further away as he walked. A cottage came into view. He knocked on the door and an elderly woman answered. She shone her light over my grandfather, at which point his dog ran off into the dark. Grandad called out his name, but he was nowhere to be seen. Taking refuge for a few hours (it was the custom then to open your door to strangers in need), he had tea and cake with the lady before setting out to find his dog at night. Hours were spent searching. His beloved dog was nowhere to be found. My grandfather made his way home several miles to Bishop St., Tuam, that night, consumed with sadness. Weeks later, whimpering noises came from the front of the house.

The whimpering was soon joined by scratching. Dr. Tony Waldron made his way to the front door to see if someone was knocking. At the door a dog covered in muck stared up at him, tail wagging. The dog had reached his holy grail. The pointer returned to stay by my grandfather's side for years to come. I thought of this story, panic-stricken, staring at shadows, trying to grasp the animal other's intention. Perhaps I would walk unknown roads that evening and maybe night too, across hills and gullies never imagined, in search of a creature that had — in time — become a crutch; a 'person' to lean upon when facing the day. On the mountain road that afternoon the name 'Oscar, Oscar' rang out. But I was also stood in the past, in my grandfather's home, recalling the transmission of the story from my recently deceased father. The mystery of being out in the Irish countryside was instilled in me at a young age through the oral tradition. I thought again of the pointer returning home to Tuam, how much the story, whether I remembered or imagined it, had meant to my family, who had witnessed the apparent 'miracle.' I then began to make my way back up the road, still dwelling on the disappearance. Perhaps there really was no one looking down.

Panic in the mountains struck at the heart of the idea Oscar was sent to shepherd me; that he came to mind me. Perhaps the idea was a way of holding on to misconceived belief in death as a passage to another place. I pictured myself returning to drive around Tipperary shouting his name from a window. I would post a photo on Facebook: Oscar is missing in the Silvermines. But my grandfather is at the table, a cup of tea in his hand, the children shouting and screaming upstairs, the front door opening and closing. Sick patients are waiting to see him; the hum of activity that allows only for singular moments of rest. The slow drone of a radio echoes from a wireless stationed above the presses by the inner wall. Grandad, a man I come to cherish, hears the whelp, the scratch from the front door of the house. He gets up, spilling tea over the side of the table. He curses himself aloud. He is too tired to be excited. He picks up his cane and makes his way to the front of the house, passing riding boots and horsewhips on the way. The door beckons him towards it. He slowly opens it to see a pointer stare up at him before he is pushed back upon his bad hip.

I am on a boreen, my father whispering the dénouement of the story. My heart is empty, and Oscar is lost. Squatting to draw breath, I suck the air. I start to trudge up the hill like a soldier arriving home from the front, legs beginning to slow. A stumbled-upon oasis takes form in a human smile reaching out to me. She is holding a phone, gesturing to say she can't get through. I sprint towards her. Relief comes quickly. She is holding Oscar in her arms. Thrusting my face into my wife's bosom, I cry.

'He's okay,' she whispers, 'I tried to phone you, but I couldn't get a signal up here.'

My breath elicits condensation like smoke from a chimney. We huddle, and the mood stabilizes into relief — he has come back again. A poor phone signal was all it took to suggest catastrophe on the trail. And the same poor signal had made the penny drop. If something happened to Oscar, maybe my world would fall apart. There was something of my father's ethereal presence in his being.

'How did you find him?' I said, shocked by the immediacy of his return.

'When you ran down after him, I stayed here,' Ylva declared, getting up from a squat to a standing position. 'He appeared over there,' pointing at the culled trees. 'He took off on the road you went after him on, before circling back,' she said.

'Oscar,' I announced, grabbing his hips, and pushing my head to brush against his wagging tail, 'you nearly frightened us to death.'

It was that one time he did something out of character on a hike; the one time he took off with gusto. A suitable cause offered itself in due course: deer scent. Deer leave a powerful odour in mountainous regions, often generating such bizarre reflexes in dogs that it propels them into a frenzy. Typical herding dog mannerisms — the crouching, staring, creeping in slow-motion — are, of course, those of an instinctual hunter. But the prey instinct, the final phase in the hunt, is turned in on itself. To witness this transformed instinct is to see a nonhuman animal working in symbiosis with man. It is to watch nature bent to human ends — culture in its fullest form of expression. Hiking in the Slieve Felim that Saturday, Oscar the hunter made a momentary reappearance in our life. Oscar then heard the whistle from Ylva. The call intervened and a sheepdog returned. He gave up on the prey; he returned to the arms of his dearest mistress.

Along with deer scent, sheepdogs are sensitive to sound. They suffer more than most from fireworks. Sustained banging causes distress. Some nights Oscar became so animated he would pace up and down the garden, distressed beyond measure. He was a crazed automaton. On one occasion he jumped the hedge in the garden in the manner of a grand national horse; something he would never do in normal circumstances. At first, I thought it was fireworks causing these episodes, but it soon became apparent to me that it was a sort of fit. The only way I could calm Oscar down was to coax him into the car and drive for a duration. It took approximately thirty minutes to calm him. He would hunch behind the seat, while I rubbed him gently with my hand from the driver's seat. I would whisper to him. The amateur diagnosis was epilepsy: he needed medication. But it wasn't a seizure. He was lucid. After a time, he snapped out and went back to normal.

One time it took driving all the way to a roundabout on the outskirts of the city, at least twenty minutes away, to calm him. At some point on the return journey, he jumped up onto the back seat, signaling the end of the episode. At home, he would saunter into his bed like nothing untoward had just occurred. Online forums were used to inquire what was causing the unease before the realization arrived: Oscar suffers from the canine equivalent of panic attacks. That the episodes tended to occur at night indicated a deeper connection to the vagaries of his past life; to those nights spent alone on the farm, separated from a human Oscar's instincts compelled him to help. That the car journey soothed him back to himself was also suggestive. It was a car journey that had saved him from his life alone on the farm — the summer evening when he came home with us.

Oscar, not unusual for a collie, has separation anxiety. Being alone is not a natural disposition. A theory of evolution based on survival of the fittest runs contrary to my experience of companionship: the conceptual *coileán* as canine helper to Gaelic brethren. In 1869, when responding to Darwin's theory, Swiss Botanist Simon Schwendener registered the 'dual hypothesis of lichens' theory from which the term symbiosis came. Schwendener was attacked at the time by establishment taxonomists, by numerous scientists' intent on making the order of things run in a particular way. The consensus, *qua* Darwin, is that a species comes to fruition through phases of evolutionary divergence. As a result, theories of pacts that operate in modes of convergence and partners are inevitably sidelined. A century from this, and a view of nature as the realm of mutually beneficial 'symbioses' has become widely accepted. Schwender's hypothesis is now seen as fact.

Oscar panics at night and, from my cursory understanding, from durations of time left alone uninterrupted on his patio, time when the usual order of the day is askew. CBD oil was suggested to soothe him. But I decided against using it. The drive to the roundabout late at night is simply the price of love. At times the crutch needs to be transferred in a different direction. In all truth, it is comforting for me to find in my dog traits not so different to my own. For I too tended to panic when isolated. I too have struggled, throughout life, with the condition of being alone.

But as much as too much time alone can trigger panic attacks in Oscar, collies, in general, are super sensitive to the rhythms of the world: to all the music of the earth. Storms are terrifying for most. Oscar's sensitivity to sound is so strong that any minor changes in my tone of voice can overwhelm his mood, moving from joyous attention to sad submission. Sometimes when his name is called from the back door, his head bobs up in the wild grass of the back field. His ears prick as he begins to make his way back along a well-worn path through the trees. I bellow out a loud disciplinary 'no' all the while pointing firmly at the field, in a further attempt at boundary training. But it is like telling off a child whose face is smothered in ice cream (holding a tub from the freezer). His forward trot freezes in motion. His whole demeanour alters in response to me, crouching on his tummy, pushing his face against the grass. A sudden change in manner — from bold to obedient.

My plan was to film this sequence of movement — through the fields and bushes home — to show a dog behavourist who befriended me through the online collie forum. Once the footage was posted as content, he very quickly messaged to say that he had watched the clip over and over on repeat, and that the skills of a highly bred working sheepdog could be elicited in Oscar's behaviour. Oscar demonstrates, he said in no uncertain terms, the traits of a herding animal. He reacts to tonal variation in speech, and he acts accordingly. His sensitivity to sound, his incredible ability to sense, comes from a longstanding genealogical heritage of breeding and training: culture-nature. Try as much as you want to scold him, his sensitivity to vocal tone makes it hard to do so. He looks at you like you are scolding his whole being. It is like he is suffering from having failed you.

That the world contains such sensitive creatures, creatures so fully cognisant and ashamed of their behaviour, was more than intriguing. One forum member replied to my posts, 'He lives for you. You can see that his whole 'job,' as they say, is his service. You're his master now.' It was a nice comment for several reasons, not least in the pleasure taken from being thought of as a dog's master. But as an analysis it also brought a degree of guilt on my part, in my knowing that Oscar was not 'flourishing' as a 'sheepdog.' I was becoming uneasy that he was retired before his time.

These herding instincts surfaced again when holidaying in the village of Enniscrone in County Sligo in the summer of 2018. Excitement and a degree of unease were in equal supply around bringing Oscar along on the trip with us, his first real holiday as part of the family. Sheepdogs are such routine-based animals; they get so anxious about any kind of change. We had planned for Oscar to stay with us in the cottage, even though — by habitual inclination — he is an outside dog. Bringing him along on holiday meant he would need a long walk every morning on the beach just to let him settle in the house during daytime. As a seaside village the main street of Enniscrone runs parallel to one of Ireland's widest beaches. It is a surfing haven with a three-kilometre strand. For our first outing to the beach, the beauty of the Atlantic came to the fore. A set of terraced cottages greeted along an alleyway at the beach entrance, beside which a grass clearing tallies with a tributary to the sea, partitioning the beach into 'big' and 'small' sections, though technically one.

A small bridge divides these two sections of beach, the famous Enniscrone dunes emerging in full view on the bigger side. One can gaze across the expanse of beach leading on to the Valley of Diamonds, a monumental sand dune that is traditional for walking groups and families to climb throughout the seasons. To the right of the more expansive part of the beach, the pier edging out in the distance, is a white castle and a section of the seaweed baths that date back decades that tourists still travel from afar to find. Beyond the castle again the same pier extends from a road to a village street, a majestic design that children and adults gather at throughout the year. It is one of Ireland's most walker-friendly beaches, and one of the most aesthetically pleasing to the eye. On a sunny day, the beach takes the form of a picture postcard. One can watch the Atlantic raging, the waves crashing or lying quietly, the foam trickling in like a whisper on the calm Atlantic breeze.

To make the most of the beach for recreational purposes with a pet dog, handlers will take to its surfaces with the retreating tide. The beach is often too soft to walk on when the tide is fully in. Dogs are allowed to run freely off the leash before nine o'clock. My plan was to visit the beach every morning, during the time when Oscar was allowed to embrace a landscape that jars, visually at least, with his physical appearance — it is a sight to see a long-haired sheepdog running on a beach. Oscar, however, took to the beach with the bravado of a child learning to walk. He moved at a significant pace from sea to sand. With his ears pinned back and his coat pushing against the breeze, he galloped from one end of the beach to the other. With the first turn away from the sand dunes in the direction of home, the herding activity I had come to think of as magical in its form, surfaced once again: the creeping and crouching behaviour. The beach became, for the first time that holiday week, a stage on which to observe the beauty of animality.

A SHEEPDOG NAMED OSCAR

One day we arrived at the estuary. It is the point where most walkers turn for home. Oscar slowed down to a halt. He pointed his nose out firmly in front, in a crouching pose. He crept along on all fours. I quickly opened the camera app on my phone to capture the movement, such was the satisfaction in watching an animal's instinct displayed with clinical precision. It was not unlike watching a young Federer take to center court. Any attempt to distract him from the white blob that appeared in his eyeline was futile. He was consumed by a dog a short distance away. Oscar's herding instinct had, of course, surfaced before, but it blossomed on the wide-open spaces of the beach that morning. A holidaying walker stopped to declare, 'You need to get that guy working,' jolting my concentration. I awkwardly replied, 'Yeah, I must.' At certain times Oscar would cease his creeping motion, do 'a clapper' (as they say in herding lingo) and stare obsessively at an incoming object. Almost as if he were seeing an angel suddenly descending from the stars.

Oscar was like a ballerina in motion; like a friend had revealed their inner passion. On the open spaces of the beach each morning, the same handlers and dogs were out in force, taking in the fullness of the sea. And each morning, a white speck would appear in the distance. The sight would elicit the same instinctual moves — crouch, creep, stare — in Oscar. Oscar would hunch, absorbed in concentration until about a hundred yards from the smaller dog. His tail would wag by way of saying hello. Some mornings it would last for over five

A SHEEPDOG NAMED OSCAR

minutes, before excitement overcame him just as the other dog was within earshot of us. Some handlers were put-off by the level of concentration displayed, but the ballerina-like elegance of movement delighted most who looked on.

An animal so deep in concentration can be an alluring sight. Not surprisingly, one of the mornings on the beach a farmer approached me, having seen Oscar perform.

'He's a classy worker,' he said. 'You see he's got serious pedigree.' A lengthy conversation ensued, for an hour or more, as I told the story of finding Oscar on a derelict farm in County Clare.

I never got the name of the farmer, or his phone number. But his talk of 'eye' (referencing Oscar's ability to control the herd using the famous 'collie stare') and 'bone' – his elegant movement — stayed with me. Oscar, he told me, displays the movement typical of pedigree. Again, the reference to 'work' and 'pedigree' harnessed my curiosity about these dogs. It was a curiosity exacerbated when returning home, sprung indeed from Oscar displaying such an aptitude for a particular job. However much pleasure his elegance on the wide-open beach gave me aesthetically, it brought significant unease; perhaps Oscar was deprived of doing what he was fated to do when kept as a pet? Maybe companionship was only a minor recompense for losing his work on the farm. The beach display was a signal to get moving. Something had to be returned, a way had to be found for Oscar to 'flourish.' And yet still, it was no easy task. He would probably need a herd of sheep.

A SHEEPDOG NAMED OSCAR

I reviewed the video capturing his movements and his deep concentration staring down a dog in his eye line. Over a century of breeding had instilled in a particular breed of dog a way of working that altered the prey drive. Oscar stared in deep concentration, breaking it to momentarily flick a look in my direction. The filming was conducted at a time when news was breaking about borders that might not be borders for long. Northern Ireland, so long in a politically controversial union with Britain, voted to remain a member of the European Union. Brexit, perhaps, the stickiest political event of my lifetime, reopened debates about borders between the North and Republic. On the beach that morning, as the Brexit debate raged in the media, my time with Oscar seemed to turn on a tradition common to both our islands, exceeding my understanding of division. It was a heritage with an inveterate timeline in the land. My dog's ancestors came from neither here nor there. They came from a space between. Handlers came from Scotland, from England. They came from the North and the Republic. But the dogs came from the nefarious: the border in between.

The in-between brought ever more curiosity upon me. Maybe, I thought, grieving pertains to a similar state of being suspended between now and then. Perhaps I am in the middle and do not know. Sometimes I think 'the bad is yet to come,' impervious to the fact that waiting is a form of grief. And sometimes I wonder whether shock is also a kind of waiting game, fueled by the desire to feel when numbed from feeling itself. Maybe borders are passageways between emotional states, some not yet travelled: the liminal spaces the grieving stumble through without direction. So, when the word 'border collie' is spoken to me, a sheepdog appears on a mountain top, on one side Scotland, the other England, nation-states that Benedict Anderson likes to call imagined communities.

It is often said by Irish that inhabitants of the border counties between the Republic and of Northern Ireland travel without even being aware of stepping from one nation into another. Perhaps grief is a similar passage. We look for signposts to signal a passage from one area to another. But without it in place, the remains are vast and unknown. We ramble, without any warning, without any clear direction of where we are and sometimes we try to stand and look, like the collie in my mind's eye, from a mountaintop, on its peak. But the peak is never reached. Instead, we must remain ignorant of its existence.

Border collies were first classified as a breed in the late 19th century. The most popular herding dog across 20th-century Britain and Ireland were soon recognizable as a type. History denotes a Northumberland County origin with the emergence of 'Old Hemp.' As a legendary sheepdog, said to have sired over two hundred puppies, it is nonetheless difficult to make out Old Hemp's tricolour (black, white, and tan) markings in the few black and white photographs that survive to this day. When conducting research into the origin of

A SHEEPDOG NAMED OSCAR

DARA WALDRON

sheepdogs on the Scottish and English borderlands, I became attuned to the physical similarities between Oscar and Old Hemp. They are both of a similar height. Both look with an intense stare. The more pictures of Old Hemp I scrutinized, the more my companion — who seemed to always look to me for guidance (and whose guidance to me seemed to be a kind of care) — registered as a 'person' in my mind. I became consumed with the idea of returning something to him, to let him 'flourish' around what is otherwise known as work.

Suddenly I turned around and she was standin' there,
With silver bracelets on her wrists and flowers in her hair,
She walked up to me so gracefully and took my crown of thorns,
'Come in,' she said, 'I'll give you shelter from the storm'.

—Bob Dylan
'Shelter from the Storm'

THREE ⁑ FROM ANOTHER WORLD

I first met Tom in the woods when he was working for the tidy town group. I was running the trail in a feverish state, with Oscar by my side, when two men appeared. They were volunteers in the process of building feeders for the red squirrel population, a vital part of the forest ecosystem. Cognizant that some people are terrified of dogs, I grasped at the leash immediately. Oscar was his usual friendly self. Tom began to rub Oscar's stomach and complement his good looks. Because he spoke with such passion about dogs, it was obvious he was the local 'Tom' I had been told was a breeder of sheepdogs. He had bred in the past, he said, but not anymore. He did, however, have several dogs at home. We kept in contact over winter and met up again in the spring.

I showed the film of Oscar on the beach to Tom, and he recommended bringing him to sheep, at the end of lambing season. By that time the weather would have improved. Over winter, unannounced lessons in working herds took place upon casual meetings with Tom. I tapped into his wealth of knowledge around herding. Tom had been to trials across Ireland and Britain. He had imported dogs from Wales. He had a vast knowledge of farming traditions across the Midwest.

That winter the sale of my father's estate loomed large, and the eventual loss not just of a home, but also the traces left behind, hit harder than expected. The ensuing sale of the house and land brought the weight of loss crashing down. Somehow, if the farm remained in the family's name, the fantasy of my father's return would remain intact. A few years after the land in Cloondarone was purchased, in my teens, my father built a house and stables on the land intending to breed thoroughbred racehorses. Against my urban instincts, I became accustomed to country ways. I was — of course — a townie. But I understood the rural/urban divides. I could hold a conversation with farmers about silage, lambing season, dairy farming. Stuff that preoccupies farmers I was informed about, giving me a good grasp of what motivated those who live close to the land. For this reason, an organic relationship formed with Tom. We had a common interest in country life.

Tom was training a one-year-old short-haired collie, an energetic bitch with a high ceiling called Nell. He agreed to give Oscar a run at the sheep with her. It was a chance to see if he had any training. When the day finally arrived to meet, though suspecting Oscar was trained in his previous life, a rush of excitement pulsated through me. Undertaking a herding activity, far from replicating my father's passion for horses, apportioned something I felt he would have enjoyed. It lifted my spirits. A scene took form in my imagination: my father is staying with us in a house he has never seen. We are drinking tea, waiting for Tom to call. The plan is to follow Tom to Rear Cross, where the sheep are. In my mind's eye, Dad is sitting in the passenger seat beside me, Oscar is in the back. We set off along the back roads towards the farm, passing the little dip and then rise in the road that signals the entrance to the Clare Glens and then on again.

I am in the real world yet navigating through the speculative world of imagination, ushering my father back in time. A film plays in my cinema mind as the car rolls along the winding road to Tom's place. The ghostly presence of memory filters through the window, slowly joining as a present. From Tuam to Limerick, from Enniscrone to Connemara, to rolling vistas of Tipperary. Fiction meets reality and the borderline between the world of facts and desires slowly melts with the sun.

Dad hears how Oscar shepherded me through the months of shock. The pain. He stares out the window at the Limerick Tipperary border. He wants to know where we are going. 'Tipperary; I am giving something back to Oscar.' Then I remember Tipperary is where he died. He was on his way home from a point-to-point, having served as a medical officer. When his room was being cleared, numerous out-of-date cheques from point-to-points he worked on in the West and

Midwest were found. 'He never cashed them,' Loe said, 'he was giving something back.' Perhaps I was also trying to give something back. To return something to Oscar I believed he had lost, some part of his core being. 'It sounds crazy, he came along when you went away. I'm giving something back.' Dad looks at me sternly before a wry smile breaks out. 'Okay, I didn't tell you that I was leaving,' he replies. He pushes his reading glasses to the side and looks away, ashamed, perhaps, to look at me. I catch his gaze but all I see is an old man unlike the image etched in my mind. I want to ask if he sent Oscar to me. But he is gone, his seat empty. There is no outburst, no tears requiring that I pull in. There is only the sad realisation that traces of the dead persist in the depths of being, long after they have left. The window is pulled up as I turn to Oscar. 'I know you know,' I say to a dog sitting next to me, as we pass by the hills marking our entrance to Tipperary.

Tom's jeep crept along a road on the better-serviced regions of the island. He drove to Rear Cross, maneuvering bends and turns. We followed. The road began to rise at Newport GAA grounds. At the school yard on the left some miles after, we peered across at the definitive regional trait: the valleys. Driving through a sparsely populated landscape, with its valleys, elongations and falls, the bloom of summer released an expressive beauty. We pulled in at a little slope on a by road, a few miles before the village center. I recognized, at once, the road as one of the old routes we cycled many times without knowing that a small boreen even existed. It was like a mysterious netherworld in counterpart to the real. It was a boreen with a small mullet of grass running up its middle pathway, marking the point when things turn to very rural, where modern Ireland meets its past.

The Newport to Thurles Road, past Rear Cross, is one of the region's better roads and one of the reasons it makes for such good cycling. It is well-marked with practically no potholes. For this reason, pursuing Tom felt something like a miasma, a bridge into the old of old Ireland. There was an air of excitement as the car rocked back and forth on approaching an oasis of farmland. It was a point beyond which the beauty of the Limerick-Tipperary borderlands stood out in their expressive grandeur. I parked and got out and put the leash around Oscar's neck, to stop him from wandering down to the main road. Once he was secure, we began to make our way to the field Tom was waiting in. Tom had a rope tied to Nell's collar, to let her circle the pen and to build up her familiarity with a flock of sheep. Inside the field as the gate shut behind us, the painterly appearance of the hemmed in bushes stood out, a field gorgeously decorated by purple touches of rhododendron. The place had a dream-like quality, a serenity in a kind of hidden romantic idyll.

The pen in the center of the field held seven ewes on a temporary basis. Tom went out two or three times a week to train Nell. The ewes were exceptionally large — larger than I had imagined — dwarfing Nell, a slim short-haired collie, in comparison. Tom took his time moving Nell back and forward in a near trance-like execution, enticing her to herd when the pen opened. He then decided — shouting back to me about his decision — to open the pen in order to test the efficacy of Nell's training. As soon as the pen opened the sheep came running out in a small but coherent grouping. Nell then ran after the sheep at near full speed, nipping at the back tails of the frightened ewes.

'Stop, stop,' Tom shouted, tripping over his wellingtons when running towards the corner of the field. By the time he caught up with her and put the rope around Nell's neck, the sheep were all hemmed in in the corner of the field. The scene seemed like a comical reworking of a scene in *Withnail and I*, when a lone bull confronts the two main protagonists while travelling home from the village with groceries. Tom, racing through the field, stick in hand, was frantically trying to stop Nell nipping aggressively at the sheep. He only began to slow down once it was clear that she was simply taken aback by the suddenness of the sheep leaving the pen in droves. Oscar looked upon the scene, oblivious to the unfolding chaos. Eventually, Tom managed to round the sheep up, and move them into a corner, holding Nell in the process. I walked over to where he was standing, attempting to coax Oscar into something that resembled herding but realising he wasn't interested.

'He probably needs to go around the pen on the rope to give him an extra push,' Tom said, 'although he might be too accustomed to the domestic.'

'Look, we'll come back again,' I replied, as Oscar lay on his stomach with his tongue out, staring at the scene with indifference. 'He doesn't seem that interested, and the ewes are so big,' I stated aloud as the beauty of the scene began to impress more than any acute transformation in Oscar from pet to working dog. I had tried. We tried to see if Oscar could pursue — unfettered — a herding life. But it wasn't to be, or he wasn't that bothered. I thanked Tom for his patience, walking Oscar to the car. He jumped up and down, lying submissively on his tummy. Maybe, the cliché goes, a dog's personality mirrors its master. I was no farmer, shepherd even. It wasn't the functionality of sheep herding that attracted me, getting the sheep in line, but the aesthetic: the beauty of a dog running in counterpoint to its handler. Maybe Oscar was destined for work of a different kind. Maybe he was like me, 'of the country but not a part of it.' I watched him in the field that day, contemplating the times I had stood in a similar field adjacent to my father's house as a teenager, my father working the horses for which I had no natural affinity. I wanted so much to instill the desire in me to be something I probably knew I would never be. Maybe Oscar and I bonded like we did because we found a part of each other, like raindrops falling in a rain-drenched puddle of water.

As I looked at an image of Oscar that day, something important about the *coileán* made itself known to me. Maybe it was to do with suffering and what it means to watch another suffer. A certain type of person will always want to come to

DARA WALDRON

the rescue and fix. A desire to rescue in this way is predicated on the fear of suffering. The fixer is unable to watch another suffer as they cannot bear to feel another's pain. I now think that my grasp of 'flourishing' as a concept was predicated on this very conundrum: on the desire to rescue and fix the other. I wanted so much to give something back to Oscar I believed he had lost. I wanted to fix him. It was only when gazing into the field, at Tom, Oscar, and the ewes, that I experienced some kind of epiphany: our companionship is not about fixing, human or nonhuman. It is about the rescuing journey that involves another journeying with me, and me journeying with another — in symbiosis. This is what is meant by dissolving into a puddle of rain. This is what is meant by companionship and love.

Oscar moved up and down, gazing away. I went to the edge of the field to hug him. It wasn't to be. Companionship, as John said, is an art of being together. I could see it. Being with me is a form of 'work' — like running after sheep in a field. To be my companion, to forage a relationship with another organism, is the work a maker had designed for him. I took pleasure in this discovery on the drive home through Tipperary that afternoon, turning on and thinking about comments made by someone on the border collie forum. One was made in response to my query as to why Oscar tended to eat his food when we were all going to bed. I was informed that border collies will often wait until everyone is curled up, the house is quiet, and sleep beckons. The house rests and they feel comfortable enough to eat. 'Work' is done, the herd sleeps. Sheepdogs are helpers, as scientists would say, in symbiosis. They are lichens of the animal world. They settle when a family settles. I fell upon this realisation, peering into the field, like a mirror reflecting my image.

The bowl lies beside the basket on the floor. Oscar stares up with gentle eyes. He sits against the wall, front paw lifted in my direction. No matter how much is there, he will wait for the person feeding to leave the room. And then, like magic, an empty bowl waits for collection the next day. About a week after our trip to Rear Cross to see Tom, I lay on the garden lawn playing with Oscar. I watched him wiggling on his back, his thick coat bristling in the summer sun. He was groaning and grunting but still not barking. That he did not bark, that he seemed unable to let out a groan, was distressing to me, and I even considered asking the vet to see if he had been operated on to stop him from barking. Maybe the constant barking was too much for a previous owner to cope with. Or maybe he was too submissive to let out a bark? Or maybe he had been trained not to? The truth is I had no idea why he did not bark, and it was bothering me more and more not to know.

Oscar's silence was part of our lives. To some extent, it was a blessing. No persistent drone carried through the night. His silence was a marker of the weeks and months alone. I was stretched on the lawn, making my way through a book about trauma that included a chapter on Holocaust survivors who had become parents. I thought about these survivors, as the text informs, who could not speak about their experiences in the camps. They stay silent even with their children. A wound passed between generations in silence. Children of survivors can, however, sense the pain — the trauma that is never actually spoken of. The Belgian filmmaker Chantal Akerman is a child of such a survivor. The impact of her mother's lifelong silence is explored by Akerman implicitly throughout her film work, like a scar that passes from one generation on to the next. It was not until her mother Natalie approached her death in her late eighties that the silence about the past finally broke off. She finally saw the big elephant in the room: the camps. This revelation is wonderfully detailed in Akerman's memoir *My Mother Laughs*. Even those who are familiar with the trajectory of Chantal's career, the scar running through it in this regard, find her matter-of-fact relaying of the moment a mother speaks strangely alluring. One day Natalie just speaks. There is no drama. The silence between mother and daughter breaks, but the event causing it in the first place cannot be whiled away.

Perhaps the trauma that persists for survivors like Natalie comes from the realisation that talking itself cannot 'cure.' There is no face-off between good and evil, no point that good prevails. There is just the acceptance of the past. There is no finality, just movement back and forth; words to mark the event. Of course, it is more than trite to draw analogies between Natalie's survival and her decades long silence — around such an historical tragedy as the Holocaust — and my implicit concerns about a dog not barking. But Oscar's silence was affecting me more and more. It led me back, increasingly, to the lost years, to what might or might not have been. Oscar was more and more a 'person' in my eyes with each passing year. As a result, I began to speculate about his unwillingness to bark as a sign of trauma. Oscar, I had surmised, did not bark. And he did not bark, I now speculated upon, because those he loved abandoned him. He was abused by fellow beings.

My thoughts brought me back to a blustery morning in my early twenties when an unruly sight on Enniscrone beach confronted me. It was a typically rainy morning sometime in the summer of 1993. Bucketloads of seaweed had been washed up on the shore from the night's tide. Balls of suds stuck to sand. Retreating waves motioned in a tidal lurch from the morning to lunchtime. In the distance, by the estuary, where the Moy meets the Atlantic Ocean, people huddled together in groups, standing over what seemed from a distance to be a set of washed-up objects of a considerable size. Drawing the drizzle from my eyes, I struggled to delineate the objects in question. I quickened the pace to quell my curiosity. I had never seen so many people on the beach on a wet day. What were they doing? What were the objects? As I approached, people were huddled together in a group. I forced my way to the outer ring of it to see what they were looking at.

On the sand, in my stead, was a dead dolphin. Beached,

sadly deceased, sand saddled the creature's skin. The dolphin looked infused with life. Its skin had not rotted to any degree and the people standing over it kept the scavenging seagulls overhead at bay. Motionless, the creature proffered an angelic half smile, shimmering in the light. I stared at it for upwards of five minutes, consumed by its beauty. At the next group, a sight of similar deathly proportions confronted me. Twelve dolphins in total washed up on the shore with the tide. The corpses were out of context, mammals but fish out of water. That afternoon in the pub, it was suggested that the school of dolphins was not in fact washed up. A stranger suggested to me that a dolphin had contracted syphilis and rather than allow the disease to spread throughout the school and kill each dolphin one by one — to take the school out in degrees — the dolphins acted accordingly to stem the disease. The dolphins allowed the tide to draw them in to shore, in an act of collective suicide. The school, the theory went, acted for the betterment of the group; to quell the spread of disease to each member. The dolphins witnessed the deterioration of their fellow beings and sensed their own imminent demise.

The dolphins would perish if left to their own devices. And so, they swam through the Atlantic Sea, to their eventual death. All for one and one for all, a cliché destined to capture the mindset of special mammals. What, I thought, does it mean for these creatures to die alone in a factory? Mistaken for tuna, chopped into pieces sold at auction? Is this what animal rights activists mean when they call the wholesale slaughter of animals a holocaust? Is this the horrific evil in our midst?

As the dead dolphins returned like a poem to consciousness, that blustery morning on the beach cued me to recall Oscar's silence. My submissive sheepdog did not bark, and I wanted to know why. Maybe his silence derived from his fear of cattle, his sensitivity to my tonal variation, a legacy of abuse bestowed upon him as a pup. Maybe Oscar drifted through the village of Kilkishen; a glorious near-spiritual animal, peripatetic in search of company. He wandered into the light, kicked to abusive shouts, 'Scram, you dirty sheepdog.' ... 'Go on, get out of here,' hurled in anger. Then Oscar, no less capable of love than you or me, returned to the farm. The time before, the mystery of his past, manifested an aura of probability; might have been, as I contemplated, the silence between us. And then, one random summer afternoon, rolling with Oscar on the lawn, taking in the sound of grunts and groans, it arose from out of the abyss: Oscar barked.

It was a sticky, humid August day. The animus of summer was permeating the air. Buttercups and daisies stood radiant on our lawn. Birdsong rang out; cattle sighed in adjacent fields. I rolled on the grass, trying, as best I could, to initiate enough excitement to trigger the 'zoomies,' the frenetic activity experienced by dogs in moments of excitement. A 'Frenetic Random Activity Period' is when a dog runs recklessly at pace. It is so intense it is nearly impossible to stay still. Clapping was supposed to trigger this in Oscar, making him more

A SHEEPDOG NAMED OSCAR

conducive to play. I was on the lawn, Oscar hovering above, and I was clapping to my heart's content. Then it began, out of the blue. A sound: a bark. A monotone declaration pushed out into the wind like a cry from a siren. Oscar pointed his nose, his face set in a sideways direction, his mouth allowing wolf-like teeth to protrude outwards, like a glacial formation set on an Antarctic coastline. Then he barked repeatedly, again and again. Before I witnessed the declaration in full, Ylva and Karl ran from the garage to ask me, 'Is that Oscar?' Standing up to explain the events, I clapped again. Oscar then reacted to the stimulus as requested. He cocked his nose in the air and barked loudly. I ran to hug him. Like a child who had been afraid to speak, Oscar finally found his voice. The silence between us was whist away.

Perhaps life's high points are totally subjective. What means everything to some means little to others. Life turns in a blink. Imagine having to convince a friend who has little to no interest in interspecies relations, that your dog barking, the bane of so many urban dwellers, is your own infinite source of joy. A dog barks and everything changes, unpacking the deepest seat of emotion. Grey clouds were gathering that afternoon, dissipating against the sun. Bumblebees were making their way across the garden, stopping here and there, before slowly moving on. Blackbirds were whistling in song. Then a dog began to bark. He barked so loud that the night gave way to day.

DARA WALDRON

A SHEEPDOG NAMED OSCAR

Natalie eventually spoke about the camps to Chantal as her death approached. She had little time to explore the ramifications of the immense issue at stake. Her daughter waited all her life to hear her mother speak, to put words on the pain bequeathed to her in the silent sometimes corporeal aporia of memory. When she finally opened up, her words had a muted effect. Language could not fill the void passed between generations. Language could not measure up to the horror. Natalie spoke about Auschwitz, but it was words, and more words. By then, words were not enough.

In contrast to Natalie, for whom speaking did little to assuage a lifetime in the shadow of the event, the bark was a transformative event in our life. Oscar's bark pushed out like a message from the gods. It was never fully apparent what had triggered it, what precipitated it. Care? Companionship? A symbiotic relationship between organisms that harvested vital nutrients for both. Maybe it was that thing that turns one into two: love? I thought back to that day on the lawn, basking in joy that came from a sudden burst of sound, thinking of the evening Oscar had first come home with us, the image of a disheveled animal burning in memory. Two years later, everything changed. The dog I imagined would attack when coaxed into the car turned out to be the most sensitive being I could imagine. It was a rescue act in one sense but, as the months turned into years, and a bark rang out from the place of love, it had become clear to me that the rescue act ran in more than one direction. The bark was greater than a break in the silence between us. It was an acknowledgment of the loss carried within our being. It was a mirror held up to a soul that perforates between us.

My father passed away on a Sunday. I received news from my uncle and had to identify the body at the hospital, after which I drove home immediately to help with arrangements. So many chores needed to be done, one of which was to rehome a pup my father had adopted before his death. Oscar's first loud utterance had, for some reason, returned my thoughts to the funeral. It was a sweltering day. Awash with involuntary sensations released that morning of the funeral — the smell of heavy pollinated air, the sound of tractors in the distance, the quiet still of grazing cattle — I began to write the eulogy, referring to neighbors and friends dropping in to see my father for coffee. Sunlight was ushering in through windows, horses moved freely in adjacent fields, and butterflies pressed against the clear exposure of glass. Memory, I wrote on the empty page, transformed instantly — as sudden death descended on us — into the singular jewels of a now precious time.

Six months after the 'bark,' I went out to let Oscar in, passing his black and white profile at the door, distorted through a new glass panel. Oscar was waiting to go to the woods. Coffee was drunk in contemplation of the day. Then I heard a bark, once, maybe twice. I ran outside to stop him waking up the house, but I was unable to do so that morning. Soon it would become commonplace for Oscar to wander into the house and bark at me. He wags his tail as he begins to bark, baiting me to hurry on. I soon learned to cherish these moments of interruption. I have come to love his eccentric turn to the wind and loud holler, as if to say, 'C'mon, my friend, it's time to get going.'

By 2019 the bark was a pointer to accompany me everywhere. He would come to collect the kids from school, accompany me to the supermarket. He helped with all the daily chores. Stoically perched in the back seat, he would point his nose out the window to suck in the cool air. On a brisk evening, around this time, in the same calendar summer, I called out his name from the perch of the back door, to hear a rustling noise from the fence beside the trees. I called Oscar's name again.

More rustling. A hole was opened in the fence, making a little channel between our estate and the next. Our nonagenarian neighbour Michael was a retired creamery manager I was told suffered from Parkinson's Disease. Frail and thin, he was mentally sharp. I took comfort in talking with him, discussing tradition ceased in the information age. Ireland was a poor and mainly agricultural country in his youth. Emigration was the natural order. Gainful employment was thin on the ground. Michael spoke of a time before television or the Internet. He spoke of a time when newly installed phones transformed the island. I listened attentively, moving from the city to be close to the wisdom he appeared to covet. He looked like an aging Woody Allen and his often-cantankerous responses to my many observations channeled the grey area between the endearing and the mad.

It concerned me to think Oscar was venturing off into the other property. It was an additional concern that he was wandering over and back at will. When he was out of sight, I felt uneasy about his whereabouts. One day Michael met me on the road, and I mentioned the gap. He replied that a friend would soon fix it. He was adamant that it was his responsibility to fix the gap between the houses. Weeks then passed and Oscar still moved in and out between estates. The gap, hole, was still there. Some evenings I wandered over to Michael's house calling out Oscar's name, only to discover him stretched out on the grass like a nude from a lost Manet. The sight was strangely discomforting. It was difficult to square Michael's renowned fastidiousness (he always did what he said) with the gap that resided in the fence between the two estates. Michael, known as a pernickety creamery manager in his day, was proud and stubborn. Yet the hole was exposed, and Oscar seemed to be spending time going in and out of it. My interest in what was luring him increased. Was the garden full of rabbits? Was he drifting further afield? What exactly was he at?

A few weeks later the issue was still unresolved. Oscar's name was called out again, yet he was still nowhere to be found. I peeked over the fence to catch him off guard, trying to discover why he was so quick to make his way over beyond. But he still wasn't there. One evening a frightened rabbit

A SHEEPDOG NAMED OSCAR

stared at me from the lawn, leaves sprouting up in hay-like shoots. Still, there was no evidence of Oscar. My next step was to investigate the hole in the fence as a possible corridor. Maybe it led from Michael's into the field of an estate that sits further on the outskirts of the village. A big green field recedes to ditches and trees. The landscape there comes to life in the evening as silhouettes pushed against the reddening skies — trees stretching up on high. But, when drifting out to the field, I still couldn't find him. When I whistled over and over from the back yard, he took an age to return to me. When he did return, he was hunkered down to suggest he was acting in subordination. He was like a child caught with his hand ensconced in the cookie jar.

I lost count of the evenings spent peeking into the garden of a home originally built for Michael's daughter. (Michael relocated when the home he lived in was purchased by us). Oscar was rarely there. Hunched over, Michael seldom ventured out. By peering in, I inspected he hadn't fallen or been hurt unnecessarily. But no matter how much time was spent looking in, upwards of five minutes, there was no sign of Oscar. I suspected he was there, but I could not be sure. Returning at random times in the day to call his name, the rustling would start before he appeared, bent in submission, guilty as charged. And on it went. The gap in the fence between the houses remained.

Weeks went by before I considered asking Michael again whether it was best to stop Oscar straying. I thought at length about having Oscar neutered, taking the vet's advice to have him fixed if he began to roam. I even thought about altering the boundaries to include Michael's property, using an electrical device to do so. But some research into it put a stop to the idea.

One typical afternoon, I was collecting the post when two feet made their way into my field of vision. Michael was standing in front of me. He was bent down with a walking stick in his hand. His profile came into view as I realized he was carrying a small piece of paper.

'Michael,' I said. His head perked up and a frail, aged man peered up at me from behind thick-rimmed glasses. He was struggling to recognize me as his neighbour. A sharpness of mind was succumbing to the waves of time. 'It's Dara, Michael,' I said, venturing closer, my hands outstretched, trying to not scare him in any way. His wrinkly hands were thin and frail, veins popping like sinews. His skin was more noticeable against the grey pebbles littered along the road.

The conversation struggled to get going. Michael's 'doddery' disposition, much increased even since we had moved in as neighbours, was more apparent to me. Age had finally caught up with him. Then a car raced by, and birds flew up in the sky. Confusion relented into a buoyant smile. He lifted his cane affirmatively. I turned around to see if there was anyone coming by to say hello, but it was just Oscar standing alone by the garage. His tail moved in sync with a body shuffle.

A SHEEPDOG NAMED OSCAR

'There he is,' Michael said, his cane pointing at Oscar on arrival. Oscar had made his way down a driveway covered, bristling with pine needles and leaves, before sidling up beside Michael like I wasn't there. A tinge of envy came over me, my dog's affection for me seemingly usurped. 'There he is,' he said again, his cane hitting the earth while he hunkered down to rub Oscar. A bond between the two that I had not known of, made itself public. I was superfluous to the affection between them, a gooseberry in their midst. And then the full-blown epiphany arrived. My neighbour and my dog were not in fact strangers. They were, to all extents and purposes, friends.

'Look at that,' Michael said, pointing at Oscar. He then said, 'He loves the cocktail sausages and mash.' We laughed like before. Then rain began to trickle. Oscar pushed up against Michael with an intimacy purporting to an obvious truth of 'friendship.' I didn't need to speak. I was no longer curious as to his whereabouts, and his wandering was no longer a concern. Of course, things needed to be fleshed out. Had Oscar made it into his house? Or had he stood at the back door? Was Michael cooking dinner for Oscar in his spare time? Or was he feeding him leftovers from his dinner? Cocktail sausages and mash are not just any food; they are children's food. A cocktail sausage is a type of sausage usually served at birthdays and associated children's gigs; a kind of food small enough to feed a child. It was endearing as a matter of course to think that Michael was cooking for Oscar every

DARA WALDRON

evening, serving up mash and cocktail sausages to his neighbour sheepdog. But it also implied he had — to some extent — found a new friend during his final days on the earth.

On the way home, my mysterious search for a wandering dog was no longer in need of an explanation. The two in cahoots was more than a tonic for joy. Every time I recalled the cane rising in front of Michael, sequestering Oscar into his orbit, I imagined two beings 'hanging out' in Michael's small bungalow's backyard, in a curious alteration of a human-animal relationship taking shape in the winter of a nonagenarian's life. Michael passed a week later. I was told he fell in his house, didn't have the wherewithal to get up and after being found, passed some little while later.

Good hearted laughter, however, was a choice response to the cross-species friendship that flourished before his tragic passing. To chuckle. And from this the unexpected took shape: the ghost of my father listens when I speak about Michael and Oscar. The scene is set. We are in the kitchen in Murroe, discussing the discovery that day. 'Dad,' I say, 'a gap in the fence has the dog wandering through.' 'So what?' my father waspishly replies. 'The guy next door keeps feeding him his dinner,' I stress. A vigorous man walks from the kitchen to the dining area, brushing off dust from his jacket. His hand is held in the air proffering a wink. Then he whispers, 'Won't it save you from feeding him?' before belting out a boorish hoorah. 'Do you think he'll stop wandering now?' I remonstrate. 'Maybe?' my father says, 'but aren't they having

DARA WALDRON

the craic together?' The ghost of a conversation ends with father and son heartily laughing into the wind.

Michael passed away. Oscar no longer ventured into his estate. Instead, he wandered off in other directions, mostly to the fenced AstroTurf pitch at the back of our home. A half-kilometre loop on the side of the pitch is spotlighted in winter. It is a small component of a bigger sports complex beside our house. In the early days of the COVID-19 pandemic, a travel limit of two kilometres was imposed on people across the nation and the traffic on the route increased immeasurably. People and dogs were loitering there from dusk to dawn. Lockdowns were enforced as a public health response to the pandemic. Life came to a standstill. 'Two weeks to flatten the curve' soon lurched into months and years. Families ventured out to the shops in limited numbers, keeping 'social distance' from others when doing so. Many refused to leave their home. I called Oscar's name one evening only to find him perched on his hind legs beside the pitch fence. He managed to find a way out to it after some trees considered storm hazards had been removed by the council. He was staring through it at other dogs. Deep in concentration, my call received no reaction. I walked over, put a leash on him and walked back home. For some reason, the return engendered an immense sadness in me. I had reason to be sad. My friend was not responding to my call. Recall, for some handlers the most important thing in an interspecies relationship, dissipated in a moment.

Despair set in. My friend had more pressing interests: his own.

'Maybe it's the roaming the vet warned about?' I said to Ylva. The first sign of a dreaded wander? An extension of the visits to Michael's house? Maybe he needs a new friend? With all the pandemic restrictions in place it was difficult to access basic services. For a time, it was difficult to even see a vet. Considerable time was taken up peering out the window every few minutes to see if Oscar was there. Each time I looked — I was working from home during those early days of the pandemic — a statue-like creature was at the fence. The grass was thick; the first draw of silage beckoned. New flowers fluttered on shoots of green. Spring lurched into summer, as starling chicks rattled in ducts. The travel restrictions transformed life, dogs rarely walked with their owners were seen running the Astro-pitch loop, ever-present on a landscape altered in one swoop. The first months of Covid restrictions precipitated new eyes; a new way of seeing the landscape.

Glenstal Abbey lay within the travel limits imposed by lockdown. But the forest and pitch remained the most accessible walks. Not since the aborted walk of Glenstal with Oscar early on did we attempt the route in any shape or form. A scenic walk on our doorstep unused. But Covid was long and monotonous. One day lurched into the next. News bulletins brought reports of deaths and case numbers. The nation was gripped with the issue of mortality, in main because of the virus and media's reports on it. Walking a dog brought an escape from the banal stay-at-home policy. Everything close-at-hand suddenly became a prop in a newfound reality. The world began to turn in upon itself. And the Glenstal estate became a vista to explore in its intimate detail.

For a period, Glenstal offered six kilometres of a cycle route within the parameters of the lockdown restrictions. It was difficult to remain within distance of the walkers and the dogs that passed us along the monastery drive, and there was a constant need to suppress socialising instincts. After cycling past the monastery, itself, a barely noticeable junction marks a split in the road. The route bends along something of a pedestrianized path at the back of the monastery farm, towards the gate. At a time when the pandemic was surging across Europe, there was also unprecedented good weather. Some days passed in a surreal haze. On others, the temperatures reached mid-summer levels, and we cycled the route in only T-shirts and shorts. Passersby smiled over in our direction, offering a jolt of village camaraderie at a time of our familial insulation. These little signals were careful reminders of a life lived before in its normality, a life we had taken for granted in our pre-Covid existence, and that might or might not one day return. Maybe in some distant future?

New rituals took shape during lockdown: activities designed to keep our boredom at bay. Older ones proved difficult to maintain. The Slieve Felim Way was beyond our prescribed travel limit, but its vistas meant no police ventured there. We would grab a coke at the shop, turnoff at the monument for a few kilometres, until our destination: the start of the great pilgrimage. The path traversing the mountain range between Murroe in County Limerick and the Silvermines in County Tipperary was a hiatus from the ongoing restrictions and an escape from all things Covid related.

But at a certain point Oscar refused to leave the car at Slieve Felim. He sat in the back and refused to budge. A major struggle would ensue to coax him from the vehicle to begin a hike up the mountain before he then refused to go on any further. His refusal took a well-known form; like the time he had stooped to 'play dead' on the Glenstal driveway on our first walk. No amount of cajoling or coaxing could entice him to join us hiking the mountain planes. I thought at first that it was a lack of scent in the region that was boring him 'senseless.' Dogs, after all, do most of their work with their noses. Then a loose beagle arrived at the car park, a Kerry beagle who had once been aggressive towards Oscar and whose scent permeated for far and wide. Maybe, I then surmised, the lack of interest in hiking was really a not so obvious instinct for his own self-preservation.

The lockdown continued, and the lack of a proper horizon to give life its spontaneous oomph began to impact everyone even more. There was no goal; no sense of what lay beyond. It was just a slow drift into the future. There was nothing to strive for. The Clare Glens was sealed off; the Slieve Felim lost all its allure and the woods we spent mornings in became

A SHEEPDOG NAMED OSCAR

something of a prison into which the restrictions pushed us. It left us with very few choices. A travel limit soon became our detention.

I was hesitant about revisiting Glenstal with Oscar, yet he refused to walk Slieve Felim and kept roaming to the pitch. He stared through the green fence. Seeing him there, tail wagging, entranced by another dog, made me sad. As happy as he seemed in my company, I felt his isolation acutely. Maybe our enforced solitude undergirded a burgeoning curiosity to interact with other dogs. Maybe the picture of Oscar staring — too shy to interact — had purpose and meaning. Had he been far too young when released from a litter? He craved company but did not 'understand' the dynamics of play. No matter how much I chased after him, cajoled him to respond to my antics, he never seemed taken by a desire to chase a ball or Frisbee. He simply had no interest in pursuing it. I tried to coax him into chasing things with treats, but it just wasn't his thing.

Oscar craves being in the company of others, whether human or nonhuman. His intelligence, now I am more confident in adjudging its meaning, is emotional: he has a remarkable ability to temper the mood. When a strong bond forms, the world of a collie can often seem consumed with satisfying this duality of needs. In most cases these dual needs are physical: herding, mountain rescue. But sometimes, I surmised, they transcend the physical into the metaphysical, and existential. Once, I asked a friend why Oscar roamed to

DARA WALDRON

the pitch. He replied, 'He's curious about people. He's not used to people going out with their dogs and moving past the house at will. His world has changed utterly.' Like me, he needed the presence of others to get him through the day.

Yes, the world changed. I decided that something more than the monotonous plod through the forest was needed. Walking the same route multiple times a day was grating on the soul. Repetition made each day a monotonous simulation of the one before. A shrunken world was indeed a novelty at first, but it soon generated a dulling of the senses. Only so much spontaneity can be removed from life before a numbness readily akin to grief takes over. The lockdown went on and on, the nation and media gripped with a singular focus on the virus. My father's anniversary came to pass, as I lay on the grass. Oscar seemed fully aware that it was an important day for me, and I was on my own; without either of my two sisters. The anniversary, as usual, made its presence felt like a symbolic needle. A heaviness, physical in its fullness, consumed me once again. I missed my immediate family: my sisters and mother. I so badly needed to do something, break out of the inertia. 'C'mon, let's go,' I said, clipping a leash on Oscar's collar. 'Let's do Glenstal.' For some reason, I wanted to do the route again with Oscar. We hadn't tried since venturing out as a family on that first summer evening, when Oscar ran away with such unexplainable gusto.

We made it up the driveway in no time, the sun shining upon the Abbey. The two miniature donkeys stood grazing, unperturbed by the many passersby. A trail led down to tennis courts on one side, and another to a man-made lake. Gaining confidence that Oscar would not hit against the fence when quickening to a run, I began to slowly increase my speed. I had to avoid 'traffic' on the track. In the distance a vehicle resembling a golf trolley appeared. I squinted to see the Glenstal insignia on the front of the vehicle. Someone was patrolling the grounds, enforcing Covid restrictions; or, at least, it seemed. It was an unusual sight: a four-wheeled golf trolley apparently commissioned for pandemic use. I thought about directing Oscar past the vehicle but, when I looked up, he was nowhere to be seen. As I got nearer, the trolley slowed down, and a man stepped out. It was one of the Benedictine monks from the Abbey, wearing a habit with a hanging hood, a cushion for his balding crown. His shoe tips peered out in front from beneath his habit.

Behind him, cattle moved sluggishly, grazing on only one side of the road. Black, white, and brown clashed with a hue of green. It was like a pre-Raphaelite landscape bursting into life. Trees were staggered side-by-side, flanking a track that opened onto pastures of green grazing land. Where had Oscar gone? I stepped in to speak to the monk. He was whispering to himself. He seemed to be counting, but I struggled to discern the words he spoke from a short distance. My gaze drifted with his along the yellow hedges that marked the back end of the estate. Below the skyline, I thought I saw something moving, crawling at the rear. Thrown into a vivid daydream, I pictured Oscar, the sheepdog, crouched behind a battalion of doddery cattle. He was stalking the group in the patchy grass, his stare fixated on the straggling one lurking at the back. Consumed by the vision of a sheepdog in working mode, I reflected on the scene for what seemed a considerable time. Whether it was joy or caution fueling my imagination, my hand automatically moved upward to offer approval. The cattle were congregated at the gate, as a tight knit audience at the only entrance to the field. Brown, black and white — the cattle in their dreamy singularity — fused into an abstract miasma of form echoing Oscar's black and white hues. Before I could start the action, I was jilted back to reality when the monk seemed to turn in my direction. I found it difficult to speak. I had no idea what to say.

That so many cattle were gathered made me uneasy. Would the monk report Oscar for being off leash? Was there poison along the fence? I thought Oscar could be out there, next to a gate. I began to drift off again. In my daydream, Oscar's head popped up from behind the battalion of cattle as he stared with intent. He was concentrating on the job at hand, like on the beach. The monk was a farmer and Oscar was born of the wind, moving effortlessly in the ancient fields of Ireland.

As I passed the monk, and thought of saying hello, I nonetheless kept my head down in silence. I was caught in the viaduct of a vision: the monk farming the land, Oscar crouching on all fours in the adjacent field. In my daydream, Oscar worked the cattle into a group as the monk turned to ask, 'Where did you get him? How old is he?' Then Oscar hurtled toward me, wagging his tail, his tongue set loose. As we ran together through the estate on that lush summer day, dream and reality began syncing poetically as one, the old world beckoning. In front, the Glenstal pastures appeared startlingly green, summer rushing through with force. Sunshine was forcing its way through grey-tinged clouds. Suddenly, life began to turn on its axis.

'I found him on a farm near Kilkishen,' I heard myself say, as the words themselves came to consciousness like a poem. 'But he comes from another world.'

A SHEEPDOG NAMED OSCAR

Someone must have set them up...
In the sirens and the silences now,
All the great, set-up hearts,
All at once,
start to beat.

—*Jason Molina*
'Farewell Transmission'

EPILOGUE ⁑ FULL CIRCLE

The year I brought Oscar home was tinged with tragedy. I was numb while writing an academic book that was published in 2018 as *New Nonfiction Film*. Most of the book was written in the daze that descends upon the grieving: an experience known in the vernacular as shock. In my research I began to theorize a practice of speculative nonfiction, gleaned from films such as *Close-Up* (1990) by Abbas Kiarostami, *Two Years at Sea* (2011) by Ben Rivers, and *D'Est* (1993) by Chantal Akerman, which involves a way of making films in which reality can seem like a dream and dreams are often indistinguishable from reality. At the end of Kiarostami's docufiction *Close-Up*, his subject Sabzian, who pretended he was a known director to a family he met by chance on a bus, returns with flowers to apologize. The moment brings me to tears. Kiarostami picked up on the story, having read about it in a newspaper, colluding with Sabzian to make the film his protagonist imagined.

DARA WALDRON

As I approached the monk at Glenstal farm that day during Covid, I too began to imagine making a film, with Oscar as the subject. I was the shepherd, and Oscar was a cattle dog who had found his essence. I thought of the trusting relationship between director and subject needed to concoct scenarios the director (artist) believes true to the character of the subject. But while I can speculate about Oscar's dreams, I cannot discuss them with him. The dream is not a temporality we can give much credence to in the canine mind. Dogs live in the present, existing in the thick hum of life.

In grief, humans avoid the present. So many daily encounters affect the mourning as markers of loss. Objects become symbolic reminders of the departed, like the first pressing of *The Joshua Tree* that peaks out from my record collection, or the shoes Joan Didion keeps of her beloved. 'I'm home,' I imagine Joan hears echo in the dark recess of grief, the irrational and illogical salutation. 'Where have you gone?' is the question that needles my subconscious, circling the void. That day when I encountered the monk, I began to speculate about a different life unfolding. I began to think of Oscar as a subject motivated by human desire. I wanted him to run in the field like a magical dog I imagined my father had sent me. I wanted to dream about cattle reacting to Oscar's 'eye.' We had completed the Glenstal loop together on my father's anniversary, and the trauma I believed had once made Oscar run off in the early weeks of his arrival had gone. We had come full circle. The fields surrounding my home, the green pastures of Glenstal, glistened as a field of dreams. And the dog I imagined Oscar had once been, caught somewhere in the 'time before,' was the dog he always is and will be: a spirit of the wind tirelessly working to mend two hearts as one.

ACKNOWLEDGEMENTS

So many people have been pivotal to making this book happen. Carrie Paterson at DoppleHouse Press has been a foremost support as editor and publisher, professional and proficient in so many ways. To have such an insightful advocate of animal welfare on my side has been invaluable.

Oscar would never have come into my life but for two seemingly innocuous conversations with friends. One was with Loe McDonagh, the other Anne Stewart. Loe told me that sheepdogs make great, if not the greatest of all companions, and Anne brought me to one of the greatest.

Peter Delpeut and Aryan Kaganof, members of my small group of filmmakers and literary essayists, helped me believe I could spin yarns about a dog, when I had struggled to believe in myself. Alan Bennett at *HeadStuff* offered me the platform to test these yarns, and Oscar's story made its first appearance on those online pages, inspiring me to write the tale in full.

Many who have passed, and many alive and well inspired the book in some way or another: my close childhood friends

DARA WALDRON

Janey Mac and Oscar. Janey joined the family as a puppy in August 2020, following the timeline of this book. Hers is a another tale, to be told.

A SHEEPDOG NAMED OSCAR

Robert Purcell and Grant Nolan taught me to keep on climbing and the rewards will come. My father Dr. John A. Waldron, my grandfather Dr. Tony Waldron, Davey and Bridie Rainsford, Stefan Holmgren, Tom Holmes, Mike Ryan, in addition to the visual artists, and writers I namecheck. Thanks to all the friends who read the manuscript and gave invaluable feedback in return: Ger Lane, Céline Linssen, Becky Watson, Tom Inglis, Tommy Bonner, Fr. Anthony Keane, Frank Armstrong, Louise Purcell, Michael Holly, Kamila Kuc, Gideon Koppel, and Damian O'Connell. My sketchy recall may have omitted more, who I apologise to in advance. Special thanks to Gerry Davis for his unused but wonderful colour illustrations, and to the vibrant and caring dog walking community of Castletroy, along the beautiful banks of the Shannon.

I want to acknowledge my family, many of whom populate the pages here. My wife Ylva, apple of Oscar's eye, for such caring and patient love. My sons Anton and Karl. My mother Mary for all the years being there. My sisters Sheila and Kate and extended family in Ireland and Sweden. I thank Janey Mac, Oscar's border collie sis', for bringing calm to Oscar's life and Oscar himself for being the glue to stick a family together in the shadow of tragedy. Finally, and significantly, I dedicate this book to Anton, whose courage and resilience knows no bounds.

WORKS CITED

Akerman, Chantal, Tr. Corina Copp, (2019). *My Mother Laughs*. London: Silver Press.

Alligheri, Dante, Tr. Robin Kirkpatrick, (2012). *The Divine Comedy: Inferno, Purgatorio, Paradiso*. Harmondsworth: Penguin Classics.

Battersby, Eileen, (2011). *Ordinary Lives*. London: Faber & Faber.

Coetzee, J.M and Amy Gutmann, (2016). *The Lives of Animals* (The University Centre for Human Values Series). New Jersey: Princeton University Press.

Donaldson, Sue and Will Kymlicka, (2013). *Zoopolis: A Political Theory of Animal Rights*. Oxford: Oxford University Press.

Dylan, Bob, (1975). *Blood on the Tracks*. Columbia Records.

Gilligan, Carol, (2016). *In a Different Voice: Psychological Theory and Women's Development*. Cambridge: Harvard University Press.

Haraway, Donna J., (2003). *The Companion Species Manifesto: Dogs, People and Significant Others*. Chicago: University of Chicago Press.

Heaney, Séamus. *New Selected Poems: 1988–2013*. London: Faber & Faber.

Koppel, Gideon, dir. (2008). *sleep furiously*. Bard Entertainment/ Van Film.

MacCaig, Donald, (1984). *Nop's Trials: A Novel*. New York: Crown Publishers, Inc.

Macdonald, Helen, (2015). *H is for Hawk*. London: Vintage.

Riley, Denise (2016). *Say Something Back*. London; Picador.

Riley, Denise, (2019). *Time Lived, Without Its Flow*. London: Picador.

Robinson, Bruce, dir. (1987). *Withnail and I*. Arrow Films.

Rowlands, Mark, (2009). *The Philosopher and the Wolf: Lessons from the Wild on Love, Death and Happiness*. London: Granta Books.

Safran-Foe, Jonathan, (2010). *Eating Animals: Should We Stop?* London: Penguin.

Scruton, Roger, (1999). *On Hunting*. London: Yellow Jersey.

Singer, Peter (2015). *Animal Liberation*. London: Bodley Head.

Stanton, Andrew, dir. (2003). *Finding Nemo*. Pixar/Disney.

Tarkovsky, Andrei, (1975). *The Mirror*. Mosfilm.

Tokarczuk, Olga. Tr. Antonia Lloyd-Jones, (2018). *Drive Your Plough Over the Bones of the Dead*. London: Fitzcarraldo Editions.

U2, (1989). *The Joshua Tree*. Island Records.

West, Kanye (2016). *The Life of Kanye*. GOOD/Def Jam Records.

Young, Neil, (1974). *On the Beach*. Reprise Records.

WELCOME TO THE CLARE GLENS
CHILDREN SHOULD NOT BE LEFT UNATTE
AND CAUTION SHOULD BE EXERCISED A
TIMES TO AVOID ACCIDENTS.

AUTHOR BIOGRAPHY

Dara Waldron is a film scholar and the author of two monographs and multiple articles in international film journals and magazines: *Millenium Film Journal, Alphaville,* and *MIRAJ,* among others. His 2018 book *New Nonfiction Film: Art, Poetics and Documentary Theory* is a standard reference for documentary filmmaking courses across the globe. He teaches Critical and Contextual studies at Limerick School of Art and Design and has been a visiting Professor at Aalto University in Helsinki, LUCA School of Arts in Brussels, and the Ethnography Lab at University of Colorado, Boulder. In 2023, he published a study of sheepherding traditions documented in the 2009 film *Sweetgrass* (dir. Barbash, Castaing-Taylor) that included autoethnographic reflection on herding practices and farming in Ireland. Born in Manchester and raised in Ireland, he currently lives on the border between County Limerick and Tipperary in Ireland's Midwest, in the shadow of the Silvermines Mountains and close to the gates of well-known Glenstal Abbey and its school.